11: PERSPECTIVES IN CRITICISM

PERSPECTIVES IN CRITICISM

1: *Elements of Critical Theory*

2: *The Disinherited of Art*

3: *Stream of Consciousness in the Modern Novel*

4: *The Poet in the Poem*

5: *Arthurian Triptych*

6: *The Brazilian Othello of Machado de Assis*

7: *The World of Jean Anouilh*

8: *A New Approach to Joyce*

9: *The Idea of Coleridge's Criticism*

10: *Introduction to the Psychoanalysis of Mallarme*

11: *This Dark Estate: A Reading of Pope*

11:

THOMAS R. EDWARDS, JR.

This Dark Estate: A Reading of Pope

"Yet gave me, in this dark Estate,
  To see the Good from Ill;
And binding Nature fast in Fate,
  Left free the Human Will."
—POPE, *The Universal Prayer*

UNIVERSITY OF CALIFORNIA PRESS
Berkeley and Los Angeles
1963

University of California Press
Berkeley and Los Angeles, California
Cambridge University Press
London, England

LIBRARY OF CONGRESS CATALOG CARD NO. 63-9067
Printed in the United States of America
Designed by Ward Ritchie

To my parents

Qui semel aspexit, quantum dimissa petitis
praestent, mature redeat repetatque relicta.

Preface

YEATS ONCE defined art by saying that "imagination and intellect are that which is eternal in man crying out against that which is temporal and perishing." [1] This study of Pope might be described as an attempt to suggest that he would have understood and assented to such a remark. To be sure, he would have preferred other, more measured terms; as we well know, he was a "neoclassical" writer, and by the standards of decorum he recognized, Yeats's "crying out" could only have seemed embarrassing. But we resist our worlds even as we live in them; to recognize standards is not necessarily to observe them. Pope's neoclassicism is important not only because it explains why he did things in certain ways but also because it defines the artistic limits which he came increasingly to find intolerable.

Pope's poems show a strong sense of the "temporal and perishing" nature of experience; in various ways they explore the relations between the "dark estate" of the actual world and the ideal visions of "imagination and intellect." As I read them, the earlier poems express a sense of balance, not conflict, between the two realms; and this sense is conveyed by what I call an "Augustan" style, in which technical and emotional poise disciplines a subject matter that might otherwise make art, or any other human creativity, seem pointless. But as his career proceeds, I find an increasing strain between a poetic manner that remains in many ways Augustan and an intensity of feeling that more and more resists containment within that manner. I call the poetic results of this strain "grotesque," and my later chapters describe the emergence and the significance of this new mode. It produces a great art, greater in many ways than the art of the earlier poems; but I hope that my treatment may suggest that the earlier poems are themselves more significantly serious than they are sometimes said to be.

To read Pope's poems as expressing various conceptions of and responses to what he called "the lurking principle of death" is inevitably to minimize some other aspects of his work. Although I have tried to stay on the proper side of the line between seriousness and solemnity, it may still seem that I have sometimes ignored the delicacy, the humor, the sharpness of social observation for which Pope is so famous. I can only say that I see and value these qualities of his work, but that I think they have for many readers obscured other qualities, the gravity and breadth of vision that underlie his poems even when they are (as Jane Austen said in another connection) most "light, and bright, and sparkling." To the reader who finds the word "moral" recurring with uncomfortable frequency in this study, I must answer that Pope seems to me a moral poet, just as he professed to be, and that his morality provides one of the most impressive statements in literature of what it means to be human. Certainly he can be tediously moralistic, but outside the *Essay on Man* such moments are infrequent, and they seem a fair price to pay for the poetically rendered moral intelligence that is his great contribution to our experience. Raymond Williams, defending eighteenth-century drama, rather tartly diagnoses a confusion that some writers on Pope too seem to have fallen into: "The identification which some critics seem to make, in phantasy, between themselves and the insouciance of Cavalier rakes and whores, is usually ridiculous, if one goes on to ask to what moral tradition they themselves practically belong." [2] Whatever errors I commit in reading Pope, I have tried to avoid this one.

As all students of Pope must be, I am grateful to the editors of the Twickenham edition of the poems—Emile Audra, Norman Ault, F. W. Bateson, John Butt, Maynard Mack, James Sutherland, Geoffrey Tillotson, and Aubrey L. Williams—and to George Sherburn, editor of the letters, for making available Pope's texts, and invaluable information about them, in such definitive form. I have used the Twickenham texts ("*TE*" in my notes) for all quotations from Pope's poems; in quoting from *An Essay on Criticism,* however, I have disregarded the italicizations (other than of proper nouns) which Professors Audra and Williams have preserved from the first edition. Although it may only demonstrate how one is corrupted by familiarity with bad texts, I find that I cannot read the poem as the editors print it; they argue rightly that Pope's extensive italics "point up elements in his couplet structures," but one can after all hear the points as they are developed by rhythmic stress and rhetorical pattern, and this seems preferable to having them thrown in one's face by typography. The older Pope was surer of himself and his readers.

My specific debts to other writers I have acknowledged, as adequately as I could, in my notes; but I must express a more general gratitude to the work of Kenneth Burke, F. R. Leavis, and Geoffrey Tillotson, which no mere notes could sufficiently indicate.

I owe thanks to the Committee on Research of the University of California, Riverside, for grants that assisted in the preparation of my manuscript.

The pleasant task of listing personal obligations should begin with mention of my students at Riverside, who have taught me more than they perhaps realize. I am grateful for the conversation and friendly instruction of many people, of whom I should name particularly Robert E. Garis, Richard Poirier, William H. Pritchard, William T. H. Youngren, and my colleagues Milton Miller, Douglass S. Parker, William L. Sharp, and Philip Wheelwright. To Walter Jackson Bate I owe special thanks for continued kindness and enlightenment when both were badly needed. And my intellectual debt to Theodore Baird is, he may be amused to hear, so extensive as to be almost inexpressible.

David R. Ferry and Marshall Van Deusen have read and criticized the manuscript at different stages of its composition; I am grateful for their beneficent effect upon the book and, in much larger ways, upon me.

Above all, I owe thanks to Reuben A. Brower, for the generosity of his friendship and the amiable sternness of his instruction. There is scarcely a page of this book that has not profited from his (sometimes agonized) comments and from my sense of the challenging standard set by his own dealings with Pope and literature generally.

Finally, for nothing in particular but much in general, I thank my wife.

* * * * *

For permission to use material in chapters 3 and 5 which first appeared in somewhat different form in *Essays in Criticism* and *Philological Quarterly,* I thank the editors of those journals. I owe thanks also to E. P. Dutton & Co., Inc., for permission to use portions of chapter 4 which first were printed in *In Defense of Reading,* edited by Reuben A. Brower and Richard Poirier (1962).

Permission to quote from the following copyrighted works is gratefully acknowledged: *The Complete Poems of Robert Frost* (New York, Henry Holt and Company, 1949); James Joyce, *Ulysses* (New York, The Modern Library, 1934); *The Cantos of Ezra Pound* (Norfolk, Conn., New Directions, 1948); *The Collected Poems of W. B. Yeats* (New York, The Macmillan Company, 1956).

THOMAS R. EDWARDS, JR.

Contents

1

The Augustan Mode

POPE, WE like to say, is the poet of sanity and daylight. Many modern readers come to him gratefully, seeing him rather as they see Chaucer, as a writer whose entrenchment in the actual world of intelligible human activities and relations affords a healthy release from the private intensities of romantic and modern literature.[1] There is much to be said for such a view, but it makes Pope's poetic attitude seem far too simple. His approach to experience is a comic one, in a broad sense; but his comedy clearly is of a different sort from Chaucer's. *The Canterbury Tales,* with their easy pace and copious digressions, express a view of life in which the exigencies of time have been understood and put in their proper place. Comedy, if I understand it, celebrates our humanity as a persistence of the usual; it persuades us that what has happened will happen again, that no event is unique. As Leopold Bloom observed upon going to bed, no man is ever the first or the last.[2] The comic perspective, which Troilus achieved when from the eighth sphere he "lough right at the wo / Of hem that wepten for his deth so faste," stands behind Chaucer's great metaphor of leisure; you have all the time in the world when you think time *is* only in "the world," when you believe that from another perspective the events of time can be seen recurring eternally.

The Theme of Time

For Chaucer and his readers, the eternal perspective was a comfortable commonplace, a theological axiom that had so thoroughly been transformed into a cultural habit that the question of "believing" in it, in the modern sense, never needed raising; but for Pope, the ungrateful heir of two centuries of skepticism, eternity was no easy matter. The poems of his early career (ending with the translations of Homer) can be read as modest attempts to find a view of experience that might have some of the Chaucerian amplitude and equanimity, but which are complicated by the poet's anxious, "modern" concern about the workings of mutability. The *Epistle to Mr. Jervas, With Dryden's Translation of Fresnoy's Art of Painting* (*c.* 1715) defines the problem in terms of painting, which gives the imagination exercise in recreating what time has actually destroyed:

> With thee, on *Raphael's* Monument I mourn,
> Or wait inspiring dreams at *Maro's* Urn:
> With thee repose, where *Tully* once was laid,
> Or seek some ruin's formidable shade;
> While fancy brings the vanish'd piles to view,
> And builds imaginary *Rome* a-new. (27–32)

So far neither the expression nor the attitude behind it much exceeds the commonplace archaeological nostalgia of (for example) Addison's *Letter from Italy* (1703). But Pope pursues a more complex theme than Addison's complacent chauvinism. The artistic imagination can subdue time, but this hopeful idea must be qualified in the light of an earlier remark: "How oft' in pleasing tasks we wear the day, / While summer suns roll unperceiv'd away" (17–18). Time keeps passing, whether the artist notices or not. "Summer suns" means "days," most simply, but the grandeur of the circumlocution is ominously suggestive.

Such interplay of positive and negative views of art's

power over time provides the poem with its structure. At one moment Pope praises Jervas' artistic invention by comparing its products with the precepts of theoreticians like Dufresnoy, which only dimly express "the living image" of the painter's vision:

> Thence endless streams of fair ideas flow,
> Strike in the sketch, or in the picture glow;
> Thence beauty, waking all her forms, supplies
> An Angel's sweetness, or *Bridgewater*'s eyes.
> (43–46)

Living, flow, strike, glow: the illusion of life is a powerful one. But the name of the dead Lady Bridgewater reminds Pope that *actual* beauty is mortal, and he urges his muse to summon each living "object of desire" to the Countess's tomb for a moral lesson:

> Bid her be all that chears or softens life,
> The tender sister, daughter, friend and wife;
> Bid her be all that makes mankind adore;
> Then view this marble, and be vain no more!
> (51–54)

Pope had already used the commonplace sentiment of the last line in an *Epitaph on John Lord Caryll* (1711?), but he does not allow so conventional a lesson to stand unqualified in this new context. Lady Bridgewater's beauty is not entirely dead:

> Yet still her charms in breathing paint engage;
> Her modest cheek shall warm a future age.
> Beauty, frail flow'r that ev'ry season fears,
> Blooms in thy colours for a thousand years.
> Thus *Churchill*'s race shall other hearts surprize,
> And other Beauties envy *Worsley*'s eyes,
> Each pleasing *Blount* shall endless smiles bestow,
> And soft *Belinda*'s blush for ever glow. (55–62)

Art preserves beauty by perpetually recreating the

feelings which that beauty aroused when alive. Pope's poems and Jervas' paintings show that although individual beauties die, beauty itself is immortal, for it resides in the human capacity to respond to a pleasing object, natural or artificial.

And yet even this compromise between realism and idealism cannot fully pacify Pope's sense of mutability and mortality. After expressing a hope that his poems will live as long and please as much as Jervas' paintings, he ends the epistle on a minor cadence:

> Yet should the Graces all thy figures place,
> And breathe an air divine on ev'ry face;
> Yet should the Muses bid my numbers roll,
> Strong as their charms, and gentle as their soul;
> With *Zeuxis' Helen* thy *Bridgewater* vie,
> And these be sung 'till *Granville's Myra* die;
> Alas! how little from the grave we claim?
> Thou but preserv'st a Face and I a Name.
>
> (71–78)

The last couplet emerges from the facile compliments with the force of real emotion, especially when we consider that Jervas was supposed to have been in love with the noble lady he painted. Art's power over time and death is finally not a perfect consolation; the artist's human feelings have a way of challenging his sense of the dignity and wonder of his craft. The final effect, however, is a complex sadness. Pope asserts the magical potency of art over time as strongly as he denies it; the alternation of feelings is held together by the epistle form, with its easy restraint of tone, and by our sense that the rather slight occasion scarcely requires a full-scale resolution. The poem is "comic" in the way it opposes to the human dread of time a conception of art as a continuing activity. To the artist himself, there is a sad disparity between the living experience and the diminished version of it preserved in the artifact; but from the broader perspective which sees art as a timeless link between the living and the dead, it seems marvelous that art can preserve as much as it does, and that there are always men willing to endure the personal pathos that is peculiarly the artist's.

The Augustan Mediation

The *Epistle to Jervas* provides a preliminary illustration of what I want to call Pope's Augustan poetic manner, which characterizes most of his poems until the time of the *Essay on Man*. Its chief feature is a balance between opposing feelings and points of view, a sustained mediation, in the case of *Jervas*, between the idea that art is a consolation for time and the idea that art can preserve painfully little when held up against our personal losses. Neither idea subdues the other, any more than Chaucer's rich comic ironies deny the seriousness of the human experiences they qualify. Stylistically too there is balance:

> Beauty, frail flow'r that ev'ry season fears,
> Blooms in thy colours for a thousand years.

The ominous appositive "frail flow'r" is restrained by the hopeful predicate; "ev'ry season" yields to "a thousand years" and yet remains to qualify the latter phrase ironically. Phrase against phrase, line against line, couplet against couplet—the poem typically develops through statement and counter-statement, achieving a final effect of poise. The tone mixes moral elevation with the decorum of good manners, "seriousness" with "wit."

The details of the manner vary from poem to poem, as does the degree of seriousness with which Pope approaches the theme of man in a world of change. But the Augustan mode involves more than poetic detail. Of the early poems, *Windsor Forest* perhaps best shows the larger balancings of meaning through which the mode is achieved.[3] In it Pope compares past and present, playing off his sensuous apprehension of the moment against his knowledge of history and legend.

The poem broadly expresses a search for some significant relation between the "bright diversities of day" and the larger temporal processes revealed by memory and imagination. *Windsor Forest* is Augustan in that it can be interpreted as at once asserting and criticizing what might be called its "official" meaning: that the poet's world, the bountiful age of Queen Anne, is an earthly paradise, a living embodiment of the ideal human society:

> The Groves of *Eden*, vanish'd now so long,
> Live in Description, and look green in Song:
> These, were my Breast inspir'd with equal Flame,
> Like them in Beauty, should be like in Fame.
>
> (7–10)

Like many passages in the poem, this both asserts the genuine richness and beauty of Windsor, the symbolic epitome of Augustan England, and questions its duration. Eden perished, surviving only in the imagination and its artifacts, and this reminder of the power of time casts its shadow over the poem.

The positive sense of the analogy with Eden develops from Pope's descriptions of the landscape and its affinities with art. Like Eden, Windsor Forest is neither a wilderness nor a wholly cultivated garden; in it the rich profusion of primal nature is modified, but not violated, by the divine designing which distinguishes profusion from chaos. "Order in Variety" is the key, and the characterization of Windsor as a place "where, tho' all things differ, all agree" points to the latent political meaning: England is an image of the perfect human society because in it parties and sects can keep their identities within the embracing pattern of civil order and peace. (The political turmoil of the seventeenth century stands behind the poem—Pope's readers knew all too well the alternatives to Eden.) But politics is only one aspect of the disciplined individuality of the ideal society, as the artfully "painted" landscape of Windsor shows (23–

28). The nature of Eden is to be more than "natural"; in it nature is transformed by a creative power that can be represented only by analogy with the human making of art from the materials of experience. We need not suppose that Pope *saw* nature like this. Rather he is recalling the artistry of Eden itself, where flowers exhibited not only their natural beauties but also those of "mosaic" and "rich inlay" (*Paradise Lost,* IV, 698–703). "Here blushing *Flora* paints th' enamel'd Ground" (38) is Pope's version of this metaphor, condensing it to a pun: "Ground" is both the earth and the prepared surface upon which a painting is made.[4]

Windsor's beauty is of course more than esthetic veneer. The classical deities are at home here (33–42), but their new domestication reveals that they are not only beautiful but useful. Windsor is more truly the home of the gods than Olympus because at Windsor the natural power that they personify reveals itself not merely in mythological abstractions but in the substantial "blessings" of natural fruition. Even the apparently mechanical invocation of the rural deities expresses this idea; Pope draws upon their conventional associations of nostalgic beauty by posing them as in a frieze, but their identifying symbols (Pan's flocks, Pomona's fruits) are also tokens of their connections with a productive nature. The grain *nods*—in Eden natural things acquiesce in or even invite their own destruction for man's uses.

The idealizing parallel of England and Eden reaches a climax in the Thames's rhapsody on Peace and Commerce at the end of the poem. Through the figure the official meaning of *Windsor Forest*—the attitude that emerges most clearly when Granville or Queen Anne is in the picture—gets into the poem, and the poem's relation to *Cooper's Hill,* Waller's *On St. James's Park,* and the whole patriotic-topographical tradition comes out. Augustan England represents the flowering of human civilization, the triumph of the neoclassic virtues of order and harmony over chaos and barbarism. And the implication is that the new order will be eternal, a permanent realization of cultural ideals.

At this level, *Windsor Forest* does not significantly differ from the standard poetic praising of commerce as a restorer of the Golden Age. And as Bonamy Dobrée has remarked, such celebrants of the theme as Tickell, Fenton, Glover, and Dyer seem much too insistent,[5] as though they were inarticulately aware of the ironies that a Swift or a Mandeville could detect in the ethics of commercialism. Pope's later poems prove his own understanding of these ironies, but this understanding is present too in *Windsor Forest,* as part of a larger qualification of the theme of the ideal made real; and it is this qualification that makes *Windsor Forest* "Augustan," in my present sense. Pope knew as well as we do that no earthly state is eternal. He had to express his very real pleasure in the peace and prosperity of Anne's reign without utterly falsifying his understanding of the hard facts of time, change, and death; he solved the problem by confronting the "official" attitudes in his poem with some very different feelings.

Windsor Forest is full of reminders that death and decay are permanent conditions of human experience, that even the original Eden perished. The glance into history, at William I, reveals violence and death and so indicates that history records drastic change rather than permanence. The architectural details in lines 65–72—naked temples, broken columns, heaps of ruin —suggest more than the destruction of English culture under Norman misrule; a *classical* civilization seems to have succumbed to barbarism, and some disturbing possibilities about the world Pope is celebrating suggest themselves. Death persists even in the Augustan present, as the lines on rural sports (93–158) quietly indicate. The vignettes of hunting have, to be sure, a static quality, like parts of a painting. And the present tenses seem to minimize the deaths of the creatures—

the pheasant mounts even as he flutters in blood (111–114), the lapwings keep skimming as they feel death (131–132), and the larks, while they lie dead on the ground, have left their little lives in air (133–134) and so are not exactly dead.[6] But we have been reminded, however delicately, that death does not wholly vanish in the ideal society, a point Pope also makes in his metamorphosis of Lodona:

> The silver Stream her Virgin Coldness keeps,
> For ever murmurs, and for ever weeps;
> Still bears the Name the hapless Virgin bore,
> And bathes the Forest where she rang'd before. (205–208)

Something of her persists in this artful landscape, where past and present eternally coexist; but while death mythologized is not exactly death, still the awful word is not far from our minds.

The passage on the old poets (with which the first version of the poem presumably reached its climax) expresses a strong sense of time's hostility to human effort. Denham and Cowley are dead— "Fate relentless stop'd their Heav'nly Voice" (277)—and while Granville is coming to restore music to the forest, this cheery fact cannot quite make up for the pathetic loss. Windsor was also the home of more "practical" glory that has passed, although Granville is urged to resurrect the warrior-kings who are buried there (299–310). In fact, no human achievement is immortal, as Father Thames remarks while celebrating his own superiority to the river-cultures of antiquity: "These now no more shall be the Muse's Themes, / Lost in my Fame, as in the Sea their Streams" (361–362). History is an ebb and flow, and despite Thames's smugness we may sense some regret in the almost Arnoldian sea-image. Though the official meaning of the passage is that modern England eclipses all civilizations of the past, the metaphor implies an ironic possibility about the new Eden. A similar possibility underlies the passage (235–258) comparing the happiness of the successful courtier with that of "him who to these Shades retires, / Whom Nature charms, and whom the Muse inspires." The syntax of "Happy next him" (237) is unclear: either the courtier is happiest and the next happiest is the rusticated philosopher-poet, or the courtier's happiness seems imperfect only when set next to the poet's, as in the stock pastoral idea that you are really happy only when the artificialities of the court have been left behind. Pope probably meant to give the country poet second place, but the courtier's joys are summarily dropped while rural retirement gets 22 lines of praise. After celebrating the value of "Study, Exercise and Ease," the passage ends significantly as the country-man comes to "follow Nature, and regard his End," or to contemplate the heavens and discern his soul's "Home" there. Pope has moved a long way from the glorious works of Anne; man's need to understand his role in the natural scheme is not met by living in an earthly paradise. Such reflection is commonplace in the Georgic tradition,[7] and Pope was no doubt mainly concerned with imitating Virgil; but whatever his motive, the digression shows that the official meaning does not wholly control the poem.

Despite such complication, *Windsor Forest* remains a reasonably unified poem, and in my sense an Augustan one. Pope was too intelligent to offer the England-as-Eden analogy with full innocence, but he nevertheless cared far too much about the positive content of the figure to propose any simple irony about it. And understandably he had no desire to weaken the compliments to Granville and the queen, especially as such compliments expressed an honest feeling that the new age really promised to be a splendid one. He needed to show the very great value of the ideal in its present embodiment, without insisting on its literal permanence. The solution was ready at hand, in the static, pictorial, "artificial" method of the poem that generations of hostile readers have complained of. As in the *Epistle to Jervas,* art rescues reality from time, just as the groves of Eden have been rescued. Pope urges Granville to sing of England's dead hero-kings (305–310) in order to immortalize them. The decay of Verrio's pictures recalls the ruined temples of the Conqueror's times, but the melancholy is controlled by the idea that the greatest art—poetry—neither dies itself nor allows its subjects to die. The description of Lodona transformed into the River Loddon makes the same point:

> Oft in her Glass the musing Shepherd spies
> The headlong Mountains and the downward Skies,
> The watry Landskip of the pendant Woods,
> And absent Trees that tremble in the Floods;
> In the clear azure Gleam the Flocks are seen,
> And floating Forests paint the Waves with Green.
> Thro' the fair Scene rowl slow the lingring Streams,
> Then foaming pour along, and rush into the *Thames.* (211–218)

The paradoxes—of reality that is both absent and animatedly "there," of motion that yet sustains an eternal presence—have their counterpart in poetry as well as in painting; the poem's temporal existence, and the poet's, do not compromise the permanence of expression. "On *Cooper*'s Hill eternal Wreaths shall grow, / While lasts the Mountain, or while *Thames* shall flow" (265–266).

The conclusion of the poem is less "feeble and flat" than Joseph Warton (like many later readers) supposed. The retreat from grandiloquence ("The Thoughts of Gods let *Granville*'s Verse recite") to pastoral modesty ("My humble Muse, in unambitious Strains, / Paints the green Forests and the flow'ry

Plains") completes the theme of artistic permanence. Granville may continue the panegyric, but the epic mood isn't quite appropriate. Pope's humility masks the belief that the main job has been done—the painting is finished, and as an image of glory it will outlast its object. The anticlimax is a deliberate warning against taking the literal sense of the poem too seriously; it is only a way of speaking, but ways of speaking may finally be our only defenses against time.

Thus the descriptive method of *Windsor Forest*—the treatment of scenic set-pieces in visual imagery that recalls conventional seventeenth-century landscape painting, with its pastoral vignettes, ruins, and glimpses of rural life more or less statically drawn—has close connections with its meaning. The original Eden, the archetype of the ideal society, vanished long ago but persists in description and song; England seems in many ways a new Eden, but it too will pass away, and so its present perfection must be captured and eternalized in poems, Granville's and Pope's own. Pope's attitude toward his subject thus strikes a delicate poise between enthusiastic celebration of present glory and sober awareness that such glory passes. The emphasis on art, with its power to transcend time, reconciles the opposite and leads to an over-all view in which ideal values are strongly asserted even as they are tested and qualified by the poet's realistic intelligence. This expression of confidence in the power of the imagination to mediate between the ideal and the real is essentially Augustan.

Heroic and Pastoral Myths

The landmarks of Pope's early career—the *Pastorals* (1709), *An Essay on Criticism* (1711), *Windsor Forest* (1713), *The Rape of the Lock* (1714), and *The Temple of Fame* (1715)—can all be taken as Augustan versions of experience. Each poem, that is, deals in some way with an antagonism between an imaginative ideal, or "myth," and a set of "facts" that challenges or contradicts the myth; and each attempts to express the antagonism in a way that may reveal a basis for mediation. In *Windsor Forest* the antagonism is between a present embodiment of a cultural ideal and a history which demonstrates the impermanence of cultural achievements. In the *Essay on Criticism* and *The Temple of Fame* the terms of the conflict are modified. As I read them, both poems explore the contrasts between an ideal past—the "heroic" age of classical literary greatness—and a present in which literary heroism, if it is possible at all, must be a sadly diminished thing. And in both poems an Augustan reconciliation is achieved—or at least attempted, in the case of *The Temple of Fame*—through an appeal to paradoxes about art similar to those developed in *Windsor Forest* and the *Epistle to Jervas.*

In the *Essay on Criticism* and *The Temple of Fame* the great writers of the past are accorded a veneration that raises them above the mortal status they originally shared with other men and in a sense rescues them from death:

> Still green with Bays each ancient Altar stands,
> Above the reach of Sacrilegious Hands,
> Secure from Flames, from Envy's fiercer Rage,
> Destructive War, and all-involving Age.
>
> (*E. on C.*, 181–184)

But Pope's whole view of the classical past is not this simple. The "happier days" in which the Ancients lived may seem happy only to those who never lived in them; happy or not, they have passed, and the modern artist finds no such consolation in his own activities:

> Now Length of Fame (our second Life) is lost,
> And bare Threescore is all ev'n That can boast:

Our Sons their Fathers' failing Language see,
And such as *Chaucer* is, shall *Dryden* be.
(*E. on C.*, 480–483)

The contemporary fear of the disintegration of the language—an important factor in the rise of a stylized "poetic diction"—here expresses a larger fear, the understanding that history is largely a record of losses.

The losses are personal as well as communal, as *The Temple of Fame* suggests. The temple itself is a marvel of rich material and cunning workmanship, and its "symbolic eternities" (in G. Wilson Knight's words) testify to the power of imagination to overcome time and its ravages.[8] But the inhabitants of the temple are statues, not people: "Heroes in animated Marble frown, / And Legislators seem to think in Stone" (73–74). The illusion of life is powerful and miraculous, and yet it is an illusion. The poem seeks to transform death into "fame" or "eternity" or some such euphemistic term, but here, as in the *Essay,* Pope cannot avoid some troubling qualifications:

How vain that second Life in others' Breath,
Th' Estate which Wits inherit after Death!
Ease, Health, and Life, for this they must resign,
(Unsure the Tenure, but how vast the Fine!)
(*T. of F.*, 505–508)

In Youth alone [Wit's] empty Praise we boast,
But soon the Short-liv'd Vanity is lost!
Like some fair Flow'r the early Spring supplies,
That gaily blooms, but ev'n in blooming Dies.
(*E. on C.*, 496–499)

A number of other passages in the *Essay* express similar melancholy about the impermanence of the artist's achievement (lines 484–493 and 500–507 are cases in point); the idea is closer to the surface in *The Temple of Fame,* in the very nature of the "imitation" of Chaucer Pope is making. Chaucer is a great poet and so worth imitating, great poets win immortality through their works, and yet Chaucer needs to be rescued from oblivion by rewriting his works in modern English. Greatness alone evidently does not guarantee symbolic immortality.

Even apparently "decorative" details in *The Temple of Fame* reveal the paradoxes of art. The temple itself, for example, stands upon a cold, hard, immovable hill of ice, for which Pope made a famous simile:

> So *Zembla*'s Rocks (the beauteous Work of
> Frost)
> Rise white in Air, and glitter o'er the Coast;
> Pale Suns, unfelt, at distance roll away,
> And on th' impassive Ice the Lightnings play.
> (53–56)

This is the full neo-Longinean "sublime." The grand, unearthly beauty evokes awe, and we are to evaluate the temple and its marvelous contents by its qualitative remoteness from the natural plasticity, animation, and responsiveness of the vernal scene with which the poem opens (a significant change from the winter of Chaucer's *Hous of Fame*). But the overtones of fear that Edmund Burke was to detect in the sublime seem oddly emphatic. The glittering whiteness of the rocks suggests an almost sinister lack of vitality, an utter monotony of shading. (I do not mean to suggest that Pope saw whiteness as the authors of *Arthur Gordon Pym* or *Moby Dick* were to see it, but only that its remoteness from the "bright diversities of day" may seem disquieting as well as awesome.) The punctuational emphasis on "unfelt" seems to invite comparison with the opening lines of the poem, where "Earth relenting feels the Genial Ray." In Zembla the sun's rays are anything but "genial"—they are neither kindly nor generative—and the "impassive" ice contrasts sharply with the sensitivity of vernal nature. There is no "soft Season" in Zembla, and while this emphasizes the temple's wonderful immunity to temporal process, we may wonder about the cost of such permanence.

Both *The Temple of Fame* and *An Essay on Criticism* are concerned with confirming and sustaining the dignity of art. But in their expression, sometimes oblique and sometimes direct, of the difficulties the artist must face in an age that seems indifferent or even hostile to imaginative creation, Pope emphasizes the price the artist must pay for his timeless achievement. The artist is a kind of hero—in fact the only useful object of heroic veneration. We cannot imitate Achilles, really, but we can in a modest way imitate Homer, and by doing so we assert our relation to cultural tradition, which is our humble, "modern" version of the larger significances the epic hero so directly and arrogantly expresses. The writer is a warrior, as the *Essay* often implies, and Pope's treatment of him in these poems shows indirectly the same fascination with epic more obviously shown in *The Rape of the Lock* and the translations of Homer.

Like *Windsor Forest*, the *Essay on Criticism* and *The Temple of Fame* show Pope searching for large-scale subjects and techniques that will not falsify his knowledge of nature and contemporary society as they are involved in time. In each poem, though in different ways, he complicates his "official" attitudes by letting in feelings that are not in themselves positive, feelings (for the most part) that the symbolic eternities of art do not wholly pacify the human apprehension of "Death's inexorable Doom," as Sarpedon calls it in Pope's *Iliad* (XII, 392). Such complexity plays an important part in the Homeric epic,[9] and these poems, on a relatively small scale, show the general Augustan nostalgia for the "heroick," in literature and life. Dryden's heroic plays show the nostalgia clearly, but they also show why a full-blooded epic literature could not flourish in the

Augustan environment. Dryden cannot convincingly postulate a viable relationship between his heroic supermen-savages and the everyday realities with which the cultivated Restoration audience was concerned. The emphasis in a play such as *The Conquest of Granada* falls upon the unreality of what is on the stage, with spectacle and bombast providing the beholder with the double pleasure of wonder and amusement. In Dryden's and Pope's times both reader and writer knew too much to feel that any simple, unqualified view of large-scale human grandeur made comfortable sense in a contemporary context. Dryden may have learned his lesson from *Annus Mirabilis,* where the shift from the heroic manner to the actual matter generally entails bathos:

> Th' Eternal heard, and from the Heav'nly Quire
> Chose out the Cherub with the flaming Sword:
> And bad him swiftly drive th' approaching Fire
> From where our Naval Magazins were stor'd.
>
> (Stanza 272)

The heroic play tries to avoid this kind of absurdity by never coming down to earth, but Dryden found that a happier way to deal with epic was to put it unashamedly into modern contexts and use the inevitably comic results for deliberate satiric purposes.[10] It took him a fairly long time to discover this, and his return late in life to the serious epic in the role of translator suggests that his nostalgia for the heroic ideal could not fully be purged through satire.

We here can only speculate about the complex reasons for such a situation. The usual explanation in terms of the new science, and its relegation of human activity to a very small corner of the cosmos, is perhaps no more important than the breakdown of the public images of heroism and piety in the politics of the seventeenth century. The religio-political battles that culminated in the Civil Wars introduced ambivalence into the cultivated reader's view of the hierarchies of church and state, ambivalence that was not to be resolved by the moral and intellectual pygmyism of the later Stuarts and the Hanoverians, or by the spiritual flaccidity of Anglican Indifferentism or the spiritual flatulence (as Swift diagnosed it) of Enthusiastic Dissent. But whatever the reasons, the heroic was in Pope's day a difficult mode to work in, and his success in scaling it down to a size compatible with experience as his readers knew it, though it owed a great deal to Dryden's pioneering, nevertheless remains a tribute to his own poetic skill and tact. The old nostalgia lingered on, as the translation of Homer and the projected original epic of his later years show, but it did not keep him from trying out versions of the heroic that would be immediately and seriously relevant to his own world.

This adaptation of the heroic is another facet of Pope's Augustanism. Like the pastoral, the epic proposes an image of man that is simpler than the reality as we know it. The epic hero exists to fight, and his battles enact on a human scale larger conflicts between deities and between natural forces. But despite his being larger than life, the hero remains human, in part, and for the reader he represents a possible link between human experience and a higher kind of reality. In the *Essay on Criticism* Pope alters these terms somewhat. The writer is now the hero, and supernatural appeal is minimized. But by his continuation of an "epic" literary past, by his demonstration that the present need not be wholly worthless when measured by classical standards, the writer-hero in his own person reconciles the actual and the ideal. His craft perpetuates values, and it proves that time can be challenged, if not conquered.

In the *Pastorals* and *The Rape of the Lock* Pope's myth is the familiar pastoral ideal of innocence.[11] The pastoral shepherd, an image of man stripped of all his "civilized" concerns so that he may contemplate the relation between nature and his own capacities for primary emotion, is of course an object of complex interest for the sophisticated city-man. The shepherds in Pope's "Winter," for example, associate their grief for the death of Daphne with the "grief" of the natural world as it moves toward winter; where the civilized man would fall back on learned abstractions (when winter comes spring is not far behind), the shepherd, for whom every experience is wholly new, must invent myth by idealizing the details of his own rural world so as to project a nature that is not subject to time: "Fields ever fresh, and Groves for ever green!" And our response to such innocence mixes amusement with yearning. It is good to feel that we are like the shepherd, to rediscover some of the unpracticed directness of feeling we thought adult experience had destroyed; and yet it would be bad to resemble him too closely, since adults can never be sure that "innocence" is more than a pretty name for crudeness or stupidity. Pastoral, as William Empson says, juxtaposes the civilized man and the rustic not to praise one at the expense of the other, but simply to see whether an image of perfect humanity cannot be made from the best elements of both.[12] Like the shepherd, we invent myths (pastoral is one of them) to reconcile what happens with what *should* happen—but our myths are more complicated and at their best more aware of their mythic content, less innocently literal.

The Augustan antagonism in *The Rape of the Lock* is essentially pastoral. The social microcosm that Belinda and her friends inhabit is another simplified image of the real world of man, and we contemplate it with a similar mixture of yearning and amusement. The little world of Hampton Court is "perfect," in that it has created a system of manners and conventions that is (ideally) adequate for the expression of any human feeling or impulse. In this society a ritual activity like playing cards (compare the singing contest in pastoral) stands in its simplicity for the enormous, disorderly body of sexual motives—ranging from harmless flirtation to seduction or even rape—that we lump together under the name of "courtship." We cannot entirely approve of such ritualizing, to be sure; the ceremonies of society are tiny and to some extent mechanical, like Belinda's watch, which "return'd a silver Sound" when pressed, and Pope clearly shares our doubts about the wisdom of so wholly regularizing passion—which ceases to be itself when purged of its recognizably human disorder. Yet he expresses real admiration for the beauty and efficiency of manners, even if they are more theoretical than actual, for he knows how fearful experience can be for people who are not (as he, the ironic narrator, is not) wholly committed to such a system.[13]

But for all Pope's amused delight in the little world of society, he sees clearly that these ceremonies of manners are fatally flawed. Belinda's world contains none of Congreve's marvelous sophisticates, no one who understands that the elaborate games of courtship can, if conducted with intelligent good nature, provide the firmest assurances of mutual feeling and respect. Rather, as Thalestris' rebuke to Belinda (IV, 95–120) shows, experience here can only harden manners into an ugly, habitual literalism. By mistaking social forms for their meanings, Thalestris not only distorts morals, she destroys manners themselves—the meaningful kind of manners which may be the necessary preliminary to having any morals at all. When the veneer of forms is cracked, as it is in Cantos IV and V, we are confronted by the meaningless malevolence of unredeemed human nature.

The exception is Clarissa. Her movingly "moral" appeal for good humor as the only possible constant in a world in which "frail Beauty must decay" (V, 9–30) opens up the poem, investing the little world with a curious dignity even while revealing its insignificance in the perspective of time. Clarissa's tone wavers touchingly between rueful amusement and sadness, and although she sees death only in a limited perspective, she nevertheless sees it and responds to its power.[14] But so somber a "moral" is too simple for Pope's design, and he restores Augustan balance by returning to the pastoral myth in his final declaration of love for his heroine. Belinda has lost the lock, but the poet's fancy sees it transformed to a "sudden Star" whose "radiant Trail of Hair," like the lock of Berenice which became a constellation, "bespangl[es]" the heavens with "dishevel'd Light" (V, 127–130). This brilliant image marks a heightening of tone that brings the poem (after satiric side-glances at society lovers and the astrologer Partridge) to a triumphant conclusion:

> When those fair Suns shall sett, as sett they
> must,
> And all those Tresses shall be laid in Dust;
> *This Lock*, the Muse shall consecrate to Fame,
> And midst the Stars inscribe *Belinda*'s Name!
>
> (V, 147–150)

The imaginative inscription of her name among the stars —a cosmic version of pastoral—confirms in an unexpected way the importance the poem has half-jokingly ascribed to her ("*Belinda* smil'd, and all the World was gay"). Clarissa's moralizing is not the last word; although frivolous beauty does fade in the body, Belinda's charm finally achieves an immortality that all the good humor in the world could not have won for her. Pope does not disagree with Clarissa, exactly; the way their treatments of mortality focus on similar details of physical beauty shows that they share a saddening understanding of time and its ravages. But he rises above her almost tragic view to a triumphant declaration of the power that beauty, for all its moral flimsiness, brings to the battle against mutability.

This declaration is, to be sure, underscored by sadness. Belinda's apotheosis is more myth than fact, an only relatively more sophisticated version of Daphne's transformation in "Winter." But in *The Rape of the Lock*

Pope is much closer to his heroine than he was to the shepherds of the *Pastorals;* from the clash between experience—the knowledge of life Clarissa has sadly acquired from living it—and love, which is impatient with experience, Pope creates a myth which resembles pastoral and yet surpasses it. In a sense Clarissa is right about life, he admits, but to be right is not enough. The conclusion, and the final readjustment of meaning it makes possible, shows courage in the richest sense of the word—the fidelity with which the heart perseveres in its affections without shrinking from the understanding that experience may value affections less than facts. The mythic synthesis of knowledge and feeling in the conclusion of *The Rape of the Lock* is a great Augustan achievement.

The Limits of the Mode

In 1717 Pope published two poems—*Eloisa to Abelard* and the *Elegy* [15] *to the Memory of an Unfortunate Lady* —that have always been among his most popular works, especially with readers who do not particularly like his poetry as a whole. Their appeal as "romantic" poems is in a way misleading, since in both Pope is experimenting with Ovidian conventions of "heroic love"; [16] and yet they do evoke feeling, so powerfully and directly as to exceed the limits of Augustan poetic procedure.

The *Elegy* is built upon two contrasting views of death. Either death is a "bright reversion in the sky, / For those who greatly think, or bravely die" (9–10), or it is a grimly final dissolution of all earthly distinction—"A heap of dust alone remains of thee; / 'Tis all thou art, and all the proud shall be" (73–74). Between these extremes a number of mythic possibilities are tested: death for the lady was almost a reward for her suffering, since it led to the reunion of her soul with its divine source (23–28); death for her oppressors is a punishment, a gratifying moral event (35–46); death is a beautiful change into the rhythms of natural process, which can be celebrated in pastoral terms (55–68). To this extent the poem is Augustan; the interplay of attitudes leads to the stoic elevation of " 'Tis all thou art, and all the proud shall be," so that the element of personal mourning gives way to the detachment of the philosophical moralist and yet remains to define the painful effort required to assume so Roman a stance toward the human subjection to mutability. But the final lines of the *Elegy* involve the writer himself in the fate of the lady. Poets must die too:

> Ev'n he, whose soul now melts in mournful lays,
> Shall shortly want the gen'rous tear he pays;
> Then from his closing eyes thy form shall part,
> And the last pang shall tear thee from his heart,
> Life's idle business at one gasp be o'er,
> The Muse forgot, and thou belov'd no more!
> (77–82)

The power of this conclusion tends to stifle the other views in the poem; "mythic" ideas of death cannot withstand so eloquent and personal a statement of death's "factual" finality. The Augustan mediation between fact and myth does not fully come into play, and the poem achieves its (very real) success at the cost of something.

What the cost is may be more apparent in *Eloisa to Abelard*. Here the tension between public ideals and private feeling has slackened, at the expense of the former. "Nature" in this poem stands not for external reality or the generalized behavior of man, but for personal emotion, those underground impulses that often contradict intellect and moral sense. Eloisa's nature is a "rebel" to her moral sense (26), functioning fully only when "conscience sleeps" (227). It leads her into a position where her instincts as woman and human being are hopelessly at war with religious and social law. Her predicament is expressed as a painful disjunction between the "tumult" in her blood and the "deep solitude and awful cells" in which she has been placed. Her nature cannot adapt itself to the asceticism of the cloistered life, whose emblems are darkness, hardness, pallor, cold. Religiosity thus has marked affinities with eternity as Pope describes it in *The Temple of Fame*—a peaceful condition that is yet disturbingly different from anything we know in life. A live, passionate human being has no place in such an environment, Eloisa finds; real death can only come as a relief from such deathly "living." But death is no simple solution. When Eloisa and Abelard were lovers in the flesh, heaven seemed "dim and remote" (69–72). Now, however, having renounced human experience, Eloisa seeks consolation by imagining her life as a prefiguration of heaven, where erotic impulses will be purified and made holy in an eternity of something like pastoral perfection (209–222). Heaven is the place where "flames refin'd in breasts seraphic glow," in a setting of "roseate bow'rs, / Celestial palms, and ever-blooming flow'rs" (317–320); the language leaves little doubt that Pope sees the pitiful tenuousness of this fantasy.

Eloisa to Abelard thus expresses a conflict between "life," which is warm, exciting, and unmoral, and the escapes from life of asceticism and literal death. To escape sin Eloisa must escape "nature," meaning both her own passions and the world in which they are immoral. But divine love is less than an adequate substitute for human passion; Eloisa's divided heart would like to "lose the sin, yet keep the sense, / And love th' offender, yet detest th' offence" (191–192). The lower half of man's mixed nature has claims that Pope neither underestimates nor undervalues; even when imagining her own death Eloisa is tormented by erotic images (321–325), and her final acceptance of her lot seems more an exhausted toleration of what she has than a positive spiritual achievement.

Pope's interest in his subject was no doubt originally experimental. The Ovidian "heroic epistle" requires little more than a dignified expression of amorous intensity from a historical or mythical personage, on the assumption that in such a person feeling has "public" interest and power. In Pope's *Sappho to Phaon* (1707?), for example, the heroine's feelings are simplified and enlarged in a pastoral way, and the tone emphasizes not the complexity of her position but its urgency. Still, enough readers have agreed with Dr. Johnson's admiration of the "vigor and efficacy" of Eloisa's sentiments to suggest that the poem has more than conventional appeal. Eloisa is much more seriously presented than Sappho; Pope's treatment of her invokes our sense of psychological reality as well as our sense of Ovid. Her specifically Christian and "modern" moral predicament seems less remote from our own concerns than does the heroic epistle normally. Indeed, Pope himself may be too close to his heroine. We know that by his own standards, as moralist and at least nominal Catholic, Eloisa is wrong; yet in the poem such standards lose most of their relevance when opposed by the energy and rich confusion of private passion. In Pope's satires unrestrained passion will be equated with madness, the reduction of experience to simplistic compulsion, and we will be required to mediate between the madness of bad men and a moral madness in the poet's own voice. But here, though we keep expecting qualification, we are not made to feel more than pity for Eloisa's passionate confusion, and approval of the poetic rendering of her plight. We miss the significant shifts of tone made possible by the superimposition upon the event of a detached speaking voice, the blending of humor and moral concern that elsewhere marks Pope's sense that existence has more than one interpretation. For all its brilliance as drama and its attractive sympathy for its heroine, *Eloisa to Abelard* lacks the Augustan mediation between opposites that is the great achievement of Pope's early career.

A much slighter poem, the *Epistle to Miss Blount,*

on her Leaving the Town, after the Coronation (1714), though in some respects only a *jeu d'esprit,* shows what *Eloisa to Abelard* lacks. Like Eloisa, Miss Blount has been separated from her pleasures; packed off to the country against her will, she can only

> Divert her eyes with pictures in the fire,
> Hum half a tune, tell stories to the squire;
> Up to her godly garret after sev'n
> There starve and pray, for that's the way to heav'n. (19–22)

This seems a comic version of Eloisa's cloistered virtue, with its boredom, mortification of the flesh, and reliance upon fantasy for relief. Pope is rather cruel to make fun of her for what is not her fault, but his mockery is tinged with sympathetic affection:

> In some fair evening, on your elbow laid,
> You dream of triumphs in the rural shade;
> In pensive thought recall the fancy'd scene,
> See Coronations rise on ev'ry green. (31–34)

But her fantasies are as unsubstantial as Eloisa's ("I shriek, start up, the same sad prospect find, / And wake to all the griefs I left behind"). By a flirt of her fan, the gesture which amusingly reveals how real the fantasy is to her, Miss Blount spoils her vision: "Thus vanish sceptres, coronets, and balls, / And leave you in lone woods, or empty halls" (39–40). She is of course a much less powerful creation than Eloisa—a belle with the sulks cannot move us as does a victim of tragic love—but in her narrower way she is complete, and the tender cruelty with which Pope addresses her works beautifully. He draws her in a perspective that *Eloisa to Abelard* cannot afford, and the witty play of tones seems a relief after the "Gothick" sobriety of the larger poem, and a more convincing expression of meaningful affection and concern.

Eloisa to Abelard and the *Elegy* show the alternatives to the Augustan mode. Each is a masterful generic experiment, which nonetheless seems to demand an oddly single-minded response to its treatment of intense private feeling. It is as though *Windsor Forest* simply stated that England *is* Eden, or *The Rape of the Lock* ended with Clarissa's speech. The Augustan poem finds its meaning in the contemplation of alternatives, in a multiplicity of vision that seems a more faithful rendering of experience than any single vision can provide. Pope's later career, I shall argue, shows him in conflict with his Augustan manner. Although some of the stylistic features remain, the later poems show a growing doubt in the viability of the Augustan synthesis. Pope becomes increasingly concerned with private feeling, increasingly suspicious of the compromises of public belief; but the feelings the great satires explore and celebrate are not those of anonymous mourners or fictionalized love-heroines, but the poet's own.

2

The Mighty Maze

POPE IS shown confronting a difficult poetic problem in *An Essay on Man* (1729–1734). As an "official" argument for philosophical optimism the poem cannot avoid simplification and direct statement; yet there are signs in the verse that Pope was uncomfortable with didactic strategies.[1] He was not a very gifted thinker, if by that word we mean someone capable of clear and sound consecutive reasoning; by accepting the didactic role, he incurred an obligation to be rational that he could not fulfill. Yet the *Essay*, even though it is unsound at its avowed center, cannot be dismissed simply as a failure. The poem is partly redeemed by just those aspects of temperament and sensibility that made Pope's didacticism unsuccessful. By this I mean that the didactic impulse (whether it originated in Pope or in Bolingbroke makes no difference) is thwarted in the poem partly by the views of experience and expression that I have called Augustan. Though the *Essay* lacks thoroughgoing doctrinal coherence, still in some important ways it succeeds as a poem, even at the expense of its philosophy. What we have, I think, is a case of sensibility opposing and finally killing doctrine, as Pope's grasp of real experience stubbornly resists the use of such experience as a vehicle for rational abstraction. But sensibility kills doctrine only that it may assert positive values of its own, values firmly rooted in direct apprehension of the beautiful complexity of actual things.

The Voice of God

In the opening address to Bolingbroke (I, 1–16) we seem, as has often been remarked, to overhear one of the participants in a conversation between well-bred Augustans.[2] The contempt for the vulgarity of worldly aspirations in "leave all meaner things / To low ambition and the pride of Kings"; the discreet parenthetical admission that life is short and futile, followed by urbanely stoic determination to make the most of it; the action, an observant ramble through the woods and gardens of the world; the Chesterfieldian resolution to restrain mirth but to be "candid" about human folly whenever decorum permits—every detail works to define the speaker and his unheard companion as eighteenth-century gentlemen of leisure and cultivation. The extended metaphor of the world as a "Wild" or a "Garden" works nicely—in its rich variety the world exists to be explored by sophisticated men of sound judgment, who "expatiate" over it intellectually just as they range over their estates hunting beasts and birds. "Nature's walks" will mean more as the poem progresses; Pope has his eye on actual nature at the same time that his inner eye contemplates a larger, more abstract nature. But what is most significant here is simply the decorum of tone with which the subject is introduced.

This tone of urbane detachment is conversational, but without any of the colloquial raciness of rhythm and idiom so common in the satires. "Awake, my St. John" is a rather lofty kind of informality, and in fact the conversational element in the passage soon is counterpointed by another sort of speech: "Say first, of God above, or Man below, / What can we reason, but from what we know?" These lines may be addressed to Bolingbroke, posing a rhetorical question as prelude to discussing a topic on which they generally agree, but it is hard not to feel that Bolingbroke has lost most of his dramatic individuality and become something like the epic muse. The dramatic situation changes and Bolingbroke disappears for a time as Pope pays his ironic respects to the astronautical fancies of John Wilkins and the Royal Society and to the Lucretian image of the speculative philosopher as supernatural voyager (23–34). It is obviously impossible for ordinary human reason to achieve such clear perception of the universe, and the consequent irony in "thy pervading soul" indicates a shift of situation. The "thee" being addressed is no longer Bolingbroke but "Presumptuous Man." Conversation becomes oratory, a change predicted by the elevation of tone in the opening line; and it is at the oratorical level that the poem will mainly conduct its argument.

This shift of tone is of course not complete. The conversational beginning persists in the inner ear throughout the poem, providing an implicit context for the oratory. We are both Pope's equals, sharing Bolingbroke's gratification at having our own ideas expressed so handsomely for us, and also his pupils, resisting in our ignorant pride the messages of reason that are being delivered. The didactic poet runs the danger of not being able to justify his knowledgeable tone. He must sound just a little like God, which is all right when the subject is crop rotation or beekeeping, something in which his *expertise* (or lack of it) can be assessed; but if he ventures upon high speculation, where authority is a more uncertain matter, his voice may grow uncomfortably pontifical. Pope often does talk like God in the *Essay*. His subject commits him to saying that human consciousness cannot comprehend orders of being higher than its own, and yet he must himself at times speak as if the whole hierarchy were visible to him: "All Nature is but Art, unknown to thee; / All Chance,

Direction, which thou canst not see" (I, 289–290). The frame of conversation eases some of this pontificality. Our double identity in the poem—as the speaker's peers and as his congregation—allows us to feel the full weight of the sermon even as we participate in its delivery. Although we take the preacher seriously, we usually can remember that he is not a fanatic but a gentleman like us.

Still, our suspicions are not wholly allayed by the interplay of tones. When the voice becomes markedly aloof and judicative we tend to distrust it, and it does so too frequently to allow complete reconciliation. Pope's decision to cast the *Essay* in the form of direct and "sincere" moralizing involved a considerable problem of rhetoric. Disinterested sincerity in Swift, for example, is almost always a sign of irony, as Martin Price notes:

> The mask of impartiality, if it were not qualified by humor, was as much a questionable type as were those of partisan zeal. Constant claims of "modest proposals" to "universal benefit" were keys to pretentious and specious disinterestedness. "I burnt all my Lord ——'s letters," Swift wrote to Betty Germain, "upon receiving one where he had used these words to me, 'all I pretend to is a great deal of sincerity,' which indeed, was the chief virtue he wanted." [3]

Pope's later satires brilliantly demonstrate moral involvement; we are persuaded that he has chosen the right cause and that his vehemence marks a powerful and admirable indignation. The mask of cool disengagement, as worn by an Addison or a Chesterfield, seems unpleasantly lifeless when set next to Swift's or Pope's vigorous expressions of commitment. By choosing the disengaged man for his *persona* in the *Essay* Pope took on a difficult task, and the poem succeeds as much in the breaking of this dramatic fiction as in the observing of it.

Human Limits and Natural Harmony

The theme of the *Essay on Man* is the familiar one of reconciling the apparent chaos of natural experience with man's intimations of ultimate order. The traditional concept of the "correspondences," the analogies that connect the human world with the natural below and the divine above, operates in the poem as a distinctly uncertain possibility.[4] "Presumptuous Man" has questions to put to nature (I, 39–42, 61–66), but nature, while it seems in its variety to embody some principle of significant order, cannot tell him precisely what that order is. Both nature and man are ignorant, that is, but only man is cursed by the yearning to know. His "knowledge," as the passage (I, 99–112) on "the poor Indian" reveals, is essentially derived from myth-making; the Indian simply projects, in all innocence, a "heaven" that is an idealized version of his known world. The results are not "true," but they serve the purposes of consolation, and the Indian, for all his pastoral naïveté, is happier than civilized man. It is the same predicament that so vexes Swift—one scarcely wants to be a fool, yet one suspects that ignorance and delusion are the only sources of serenity in a world which will not bear too much scrutiny.

Pope will not settle, however, for this view in its purest, most desperate form. Analogy *can* give a general sense of man's place in the scheme; man cannot look directly upward to the ultimate source of order, but he can look downward and make metaphors for his own lot from the relationships he perceives in the lower orders of the Scale of Being. But metaphor was not knowledge to the post-Hobbesian mind, and a steady skeptical undercurrent qualifies Pope's dogmatism. To assume, as Whitehead did, that Pope "was untroubled by the great perplexity which haunts the modern world," that he was "confident that the enlightened methods of modern science provided a plan adequate as a map of the 'mighty maze,'" [5] is to ignore the complexity of Pope's view, as the lines on Newton (II, 31–38) show. Newton could answer all questions except the most important ones, those that concern the "movement of his Mind," "his own beginning, or his end." The irony places science in the right human perspective—Newton's unfolding of natural law must be contemplated in relation to his inability even to "describe," much less "explain," his own position in a universe of time and change.

This criticism of "reason" becomes explicit in the rest of Epistle II. It is a mistake to view the poem through the Victorian lens of "an age of prose and reason." As Professor Lovejoy observes, the most influential authors of the eighteenth century

> made a great point of reducing man's claims to "reason" to a minimum, and of belittling the importance of the faculty in human existence; and the vice of "pride" which they so delighted to castigate was exemplified for them in any high estimate of the capacity of the human species for intellectual achievement, or in any of the more ambitious enterprises of science and philosophy, or in any moral idea which would make pure reason (as distinguished from natural "passions") the supreme power in human life.[6]

One of the strongest forces drawing Pope away from a simple confidence in reason is his understanding that like any human faculty, it operates within the confines of "the lurking principle of death" (II, 134). The phrase appears only as a simile within a passage whose main subject is the power of a "ruling passion" to undermine mental health; but the idea of life being a gradual dying reminds us of that area of the whole scheme which reason cannot investigate. Reason has its value, but Pope takes the Platonic view of it as "guard," not "guide" (II, 162), in a world whose springs of action are passionate.

In short, all that man can know about the processes of time and change are their fragmentary effects on nature and himself. His sense of his own identity, which he yearns to define in relation to these processes, must remain disconnected and dim. There is thus a tragic paradox in Pope's use of the Scale of Being, which has lost its former metaphoric potency as a true ladder by which man might transcend his earthly condition.[7] The concept suggests that man is a part of a cosmic perfection, but he can never experience that perfection while he remains man. The problem for the moralist lay in man's discontent with his lot. If it is a condition of his middle status, how can he be censured for feeling discontent? And yet, the whole tenor of the poem insists, it is disastrous to him to feel it! Analogy is not a solution; to know something by analogy is painfully unlike knowing it by experience, and it is for experience of perfection that man yearns.[8] But Pope's job in the *Essay* is to forbid despair; he evades this impasse, not very consistently, by occasionally giving ground before the theological pressure that bears on his position: "Hope humbly then; with trembling pinions soar; / Wait the great teacher Death, and God adore!" (I, 91–92). While one may "adore" perfection in this world, only in some world to come can one *know* it—if then.

Such difficulties in defining the ultimate reality lead Pope's sermon to its essentially negative center. Whatever man should be in this world, he should at least not be proud. He is neither the center nor the master of nature. The dangers of pride are clear in I, 131–140, where the ironies rebuke the arrogant anthropocentrism of supposing that the creation exists to serve man and mirror his feelings; it is equally clear in this fine "anti-pastoral" passage:

> Is it for thee the lark ascends and sings?
> Joy tunes his voice, joy elevates his wings:
> Is it for thee the linnet pours his throat?

Loves of his own and raptures swell the
note . . .
The hog, that plows not nor obeys thy call,
Lives on the labours of this lord of all.

(III, 31–42)

The couplets play off the imagined nature invented by human pride against the real nature which exists as much for its own purposes as for man's. The natural world is full of life and feeling, but it is independent of "this lord of all." But there are consolations in man's position:

. . . he only knows,
And helps, another creature's wants and woes.
Say, will the falcon, stooping from above,
Smit with her varying plumage, spare the
dove?
Admires the jay the insect's gilded wings?
Or hears the hawk when Philomela sings?

(III, 51–56)

Nature is not responsive to man, but man is responsive to nature in a way that no merely natural creature can be. Through his unique gifts of compassion and esthetic appreciation he can penetrate into nature and so in a sense participate in it. He achieves a moral dignity that no other creature can have, but by submitting to, not dominating over, the rest of creation. He is in fact a part of nature, though not in the way he would like to be. He is "Fix'd like a plant on his peculiar spot, / To draw nutrition, propagate, and rot" (II, 63–64). While his place in the Scale involves painful complexities of feeling from which the lower orders are free, he can nonetheless relate his own life and death to the rhythms of nature. The simile denies man's cherished illusions of freedom, even as it offers compensation in vegetable simplicity. Although reason distinguishes man from the other creatures, the "fruits" of virtue grow from "savage stocks" (II, 181–184)—the "wild Nature" working at man's roots is ultimately the same nature that gives productive life (and death) to the nonhuman creation.

The analogies of nature thus point down and not up. Man will find his place in the scheme not by yearning for higher status but by accepting his relationship with the lower creatures. Still, to know that man and nature are parts of a single order is not to resolve man's yearning for a direct, intimate bond with the things of this world. In Epistle III Pope postulates such a bond, in the pastoral innocence of Eden or the Golden Age from which man fell. Despite Hobbes, "the state of Nature was the reign of God" (148). Human history has represented a decline from this primal perfection, as man created the social arts, commerce, secular government, and ultimately tyranny and superstition through the exercise of reason. These inventions stemmed from natural promptings (171 ff.) to imitate the lower creatures, and thus were not originally wrong; the turning point, the beginning of man's alienation from nature, came when superstition replaced "charity" with "zeal" (261) and secular power no longer had to reflect a spiritual order that was fundamentally benevolent. Faced with such chaos, man was "Forc'd into virtue thus by Self-defence" (279); through the inspired examples of the poet and the lawgiver the "shadow," if not the "image," of true divinity was rediscovered (288), and secular organization again became a metaphor for the great hierarchy of nature. The pyramids of "Beast, Man, or Angel" and of "Servant, Lord, or King" (302) regained their congruence, with each order topped by the single point which is God.

Epistle III does not of course afford a very satisfying account of moral history. Nor is it poetically the strongest section of the *Essay*. Some of Pope's metaphors ring false; how true is it to say, for instance, that the "Ant's republic" provided a model for human society, or even (reading not historically but "mythically," as we probably should) that it affords a very enlightening analogy? Pope has his difficulties in leading the poem in a positive direction, for all the assurance of his tone. Yet in the great passage (283–302) on social harmony he comes as close as he can to solving the problem of the whole poem, through an Augustan appeal to the traditional concept of the *concordia discors.* Harmony is simply a special condition of discordance, and as Maynard Mack observes, the metaphor's power in the *Essay* stems from a doubleness associated with the figure from earliest classical times: "the image brought together in one perspective man's present suffering and his faith, the partial and the whole views; [and suggested] that in some higher dialectic than men could grasp the thesis and antithesis of experienced evil would be resolved." [9] One may wish that the image were more solidly developed out of the argument of Epistle III, but its power is undeniable. The stability of even the best human society resides in a rather precarious balance of stresses, but that even a limited harmony is conceivable in the secular world consoles us if we take that harmony as an echo, however faint, of the grand but unhearable cosmic composition. The original intimacy of man and nature vanished when man lost his innocence, but in a social order that is properly attuned to the order of nature, a measure of intimacy can be restored.

The Power of Time

This is as close as the *Essay* comes to expressing anything like "optimism" in our ordinary sense of the word. It is not very close, we see, when we ponder Pope's implicit comparison of the poem with *Paradise Lost.* The Fall of Man was marked by his subjugation to Sin and Death, which is to say to *time* and its fundamental enmity to human value. It is the fact of time, Professor Lovejoy argues, that ultimately invalidates the concept of the Scale of Being:

> A world of time and change . . . is a world which can neither be deduced from nor recon-

ciled with the postulate that existence is the expression and consequence of a system of "eternal" and "necessary" truths inherent in the very logic of being. Since such a system could manifest itself only in a static and constant world, and since empirical reality is not static and constant, the "image" (as Plato called it) does not correspond with the supposed "model" and cannot be explained by it. *Any* change whereby nature at one time contains other things or more things than it contains at another time is fatal to the principle of sufficient reason.[10]

Milton reconciles a temporal world to cosmic immutability by appealing to the orthodox concept of Redemption: because of the sacrifice of Christ, man can look forward to an eventual translation out of time into a realm of being which is perfectly changeless. The *Essay on Man* seems at times to yield to theological pressure, but Pope must generally exclude specific Christian doctrine. Whether or not he believed in the redemption of souls, in the *Essay* his subject is not eternity, which cannot be known, but this world and how to endure it. And the possibilities of earthly experience seem far from cheerful.

Epistle IV is especially rich in allusions to death, which (93–130) strikes capriciously, without regard for "justice." Even though by Pope's time the idea of an impersonal, mechanistic universe must have seemed considerably less terrible than it had to Shakespeare or Donne, the concept still could not have been a very comfortable one to entertain. Pope in fact does not entertain it fully; his rhetoric is addressed to the enormous task of making natural impersonality a source of comfort. Falkland, Turenne, and Sidney did not die *because* they were virtuous; nature cannot recognize either virtue or vice. But because the universe does not observe moral law, as men know it, does not mean that it obeys *no* law: "Think we, like some weak Prince, th'

Eternal Cause / Prone for his fav'rites to reverse his laws?" The answer is "no"—the analogy of earthly order to supernal points out the weakness of the former only to assert the consoling perfection of the latter.

But this appeal to the "externalist pathos," the emotional power of the idea of immutability upon man's sense of his own involvement in time,[11] cannot fully subdue the sobering fact of human mortality:

> What's Fame? a fancy'd life in others breath,
> A thing beyond us, ev'n before our death.
> Just what you hear, you have, and what's unknown
> The same (my Lord) if Tully's or your own.
> All that we feel of it begins and ends
> In the small circle of our foes or friends.
> (IV, 237–242)

In this paraphrase of *The Temple of Fame* (505–508) Pope again sees personal fame as sorry compensation for the necessity of dying. The lines, to be sure, state a positive view of personal relations, which Pope always cherished: "The only pleasure which any one either of high or low rank must depend upon receiving," he wrote to Ralph Allen, "is in the Candour or Partiality of Friends and that Smaller Circle we are conversant in." [12] But this is tacit recognition that the pleasures of friendship are fleeting; they are valuable, they are in fact all that one has, but like everything else they will soon pass. Nor is wisdom any more reliable. When Pope returns to gentlemanly conversation (IV, 259–268) with Bolingbroke, it is only to place rueful emphasis on the futility of "Parts superior." Wisdom leads finally to frustration and loneliness:

> Truths would you teach, or save a sinking land?
> All fear, none aid you, and few understand.
> Painful preheminence! yourself to view
> Above life's weakness, and its comforts too.

As wise man, Bolingbroke stands as symbol of man's

dissatisfaction with his mixed nature and his ambiguous role in creation. The cost of intelligence is fearfully high: " 'Tis but to know how little can be known."

Hierarchy and Experience

The description of Bolingbroke has implications for the reader as well. Pope's rhetorical aim has been to put us in Bolingbroke's position, to improve our understanding so as to reveal how limited understanding must be. It is flattering to be admitted to such company, but the reader's new point of view is a difficult one—the "optimism" of the poem involves a serious recognition of its own limitations and of the oppositions that are all too likely to overcome it. But Pope's "official" theme will not permit so complex a view to prevail, and this inhibition leads to a crucial poetic difficulty. In Section vi of Epistle IV he undertakes to demolish "the false scale of Happiness" that prevents most men from understanding their roles in the true scale of Being. "External goods" cannot prevent "human Infelicity"—"the perfection of Virtue and Happiness consists in a conformity to the ORDER of PROVIDENCE here, and a resignation to it here and hereafter." [13] The trouble is that the false scale, since one knows it through immediate experience, lends itself more readily to poetic particularization than does the hypothetical, unexperienced "true" hierarchy.

The *Essay* both faces up to the difficult facts of human experience and attempts to make them bearable by assigning them functions in a hierarchical order. An appeal to hierarchy draws its rhetorical power from the useful changes of name that are made possible, and we note that Pope's arguments usually hinge on such redefinition:

> Respecting Man, whatever wrong we call,
> May, must be right, as relative to all.
>
> (I, 51–52)

> Cease then, nor ORDER Imperfection name.
>
> (I, 281)

All Nature is but Art, unknown to thee.
(I, 289)

Modes of Self-love the Passions we may call.
(II, 93)

Know then this truth (enough for Man to
know)
"Virtue alone is Happiness below."
(IV, 309–310)

Man, that is to say, tends to call things by their "wrong" names, and in so doing he confirms his own unhappiness, since he cannot make his vocabulary jibe with any consoling conceptual scheme of order. God, however, calls things by their "right" names. If man can translate his words for experiences into a vocabulary that fits an imaginative hierarchy extending beyond the limits of his knowledge, most of his anxiety about the human condition will turn out to have been the result of terminological muddles.

Like any example of sophisticated rhetoric, then, the *Essay* draws much of its persuasive force from a view of language that is fundamentally magical. The translation of our names for experiences into a new vocabulary is a therapeutic act, for to change the name is to change the "fact"—or at least to make it bearable—by providing a new context of ideas and feelings in which to contemplate it. Pope again is God, for he knows the right names. At the same time, however, this transformation of terms adds to our sense that the poem is "enclosed" by the speaking voice of an individual human being with whom we have a particular social relationship. The semantic shifts appeal to common sense: we share with Pope a firm identity within a community of intelligence and taste, and so he can confidently invite us to agree with him about names, since a defining characteristic of a community is the mutual acceptance of "proper" vocabularies. For example, we share his amusement at the Neo-Platonists who call "quitting sense" "imitating God" (II, 26). Like "Eastern priests," they are somehow exotic, not a part of the community, and his manner of addressing us defines us as persons who share his belief that "sense" plays a vital part in any activity, religion not excepted. Once we have agreed about the right name for one kind of experience, we are inclined to accept the speaker's judgment about names in cases which are further from communal assumptions. Although the tone of such transformations is usually didactic, it is softened by our sense that we have come to occupy much the same ground from which Pope speaks.

But Pope's appeal to an explicit hierarchy of values involves him in poetic difficulties. In the *Essay* he expresses the complexity of human experience in a world that is at best indifferent to man; but he also attempts to resolve complexity into simplicity by relating experience to a predefined system of absolute values. In passages like Pride's speech in Epistle I (131–164) there is no poetic problem, since the "right" attitude is developed out of an initial "wrong" view which is nevertheless fairly (even beautifully) expressed. Both complexity and simplicity are there, in the verse, and the adjustment between them is dramatized as argument. But as the poem draws to its close, Pope must increasingly derogate the false scale in order to emphasize the finality of the true one, as in the passage (IV, 361–372) on the need for human love to "rise from Individual to the Whole":

> Self-love but serves the virtuous mind to wake,
> As the small pebble stirs the peaceful lake;
> The centre mov'd, a circle strait succeeds,
> Another still, and still another spreads,
> Friend, parent, neighbor, first it will embrace,
> His country next, and next all human race. . . .

Pope has no better luck than any other eighteenth-century moralist in bridging the gap between self-love and social. The metaphor seems arbitrary—Addison would have called the play on "wake" and "stir" an example of false wit, dependent upon "resemblance of words" rather than of ideas,[14] and there is nothing else to persuade us that self-love and pebbles are analogous —and it seems positively muddled unless we exclude the entire metaphorical vehicle from the "it" which embraces friends, parents, and the like. This passage is the climax of Pope's final affirmation of the true scale, and it simply does not work when we measure it against the Johnsonian description of the fate of the worldly (IV, 289–308), the great "glory, jest, and riddle" section that begins Epistle II, or any of the other passages in which Pope treats human experience with full respect for its complexity. When he rises from the individual to the whole something unfortunate happens to his verse.

The trouble seems due not only to Pope's weakness in rational argument but also to the nature of his subject. Whitehead said that both the Greek and medieval Christian views of nature were essentially "dramatic," which is to say they supposed a nature that worked toward purposes which could in some way be understood by human beings and that included human experience in its operation.[15] The nature Pope has to work with is a very different one. He can deal dramatically with experiential reality in all its complexity, but in the *Essay* he must also transcend experience to knowledge of permanence and order; and since his "climate of opinion" presupposes a cosmos which is not dramatic but mechanistic, and thus largely foreign to human experience, his invocations of supernatural order are seldom fully convincing. When he can find in the natural world some evidence of the Scale—when he deals (as in I, 207–280) with the "esthetic" order his senses perceive—the *Essay* achieves its great poetic triumphs by fusing rhetoric and imaginative particularity. At such moments metaphor functions meaningfully, for the grand tenor is elucidated by solidly realized vehicles. But when natural experience is left behind in the attempt to prove that one knows what one insists is beyond knowledge, an attempt that must rely on rhetoric alone, the *Essay* loses much of its power. Mechanism is not only unattractive as an idea, it is also nearly impossible to dramatize in experiential terms. It is immediate experience that sustains Pope's Augustan mediations, and when doctrinal considerations exert their thinning or confusing tendencies on the experiential vehicle, he shows his weakness in the kind of poetic reasoning that a Dryden or a Wordsworth might bring off. His tendency to resort to conventional pietism illustrates this weakness. He tries to soften the concept of mechanism by hinting that the Christian God is at the controls, but this scrambles his argument; for example, at the end of the poem, when he declares that virtue is not only the sole source of earthly happiness but also a way to ascend to God, we uneasily feel that he has come close to contradicting his earlier assertion that the quality of human life, *as man knows it,* has no relevance to the ultimate reality. But the main problem is a literary and not just a logical one. It is not that Pope tries to make us know what he himself has called unknowable, but that the quality of the knowledge we receive is flawed by his inability to manage an abstract poetic idiom. When he treats the "true Scale" his language is less rich, less interesting, and above all less intelligible than when he expresses the perplexing imperfections of actual experience. His sensibility was attuned to the concrete, the immediate, and the *Essay* is not fully alive at the moments when its oratory loses touch with natural particulars.

The poem finally seems most interesting when read not as philosophy but as an expression of a conflict between views of reality as excitingly terrible and as ultimately orderly and peaceful. In such a reading one sees Pope as a man whose strong sense of the value of order makes experienced disorder a dreadful thing to consider, and who yearns for an imaginative myth of cosmic immutability to sustain and console him. The myth does not work perfectly, to be sure; when the poetic speaker invokes a hierarchy that he has not fully grasped imaginatively, the poem falters, regaining its stride only when he returns to the world he can experience directly. But another kind of drama emerges from this conflict of experience and speculation, a drama in which a human being tries out ways of coming to terms with his situation and finds that though none are entirely adequate some work better than others. A man who was wholly convinced by his own vision of order would not need to test it so often against actuality; Pope's poetic concern for real things and real feelings (another way of saying his humanity) refuses to surrender to his speculations, and the result is poetry. The poetry is intermittent, to be sure. When Mr. Mack calls the *Essay on Man* the greatest speculative poem in English between *Paradise Lost* and *The Prelude,*[16] we think as much of the decline such poetry suffered in the eighteenth century as of Pope's achievement. No one could deny that the poem would be better if its argument were more consistently reasoned, if the didactic impulse were more cogently realized. But such "intentional" success would have taken the *Essay* even further from the Augustan mode's complex adjustment of ideal and actual, and the poem's poetic failure is the curious measure of its human success.

3

Nature as Moral Norm

THE *Moral Essays* show Pope adapting his Augustan manner to the service of a broader variety of subjects and attitudes. The change is first of all a change of voice, from the God-like oratory of the *Essay on Man* to the witty informality of (for example) the opening of the *Epistle to Bathurst:* "Who shall decide, when Doctors disagree, / And soundest Casuists doubt, like you and me?" When, a few lines later, Pope adds to his professed optimism about human nature the parenthetical remark that "surely, Heav'n and I are of a mind," we see how far we have come. The speaker in the *Essay on Man* was often "of a mind" with heaven, but he never treated the analogy between himself and God lightly. In *Bathurst,* however, the analogy becomes a joke; we are to feel the presence not of God but of a witty human intelligence that does not stand upon its own dignity. The poet's "authority" is projected in social terms, not as a demand for an act of faith. Each of the four *Moral Essays* begins in this conversational way, implying that something—chats about books, women, human nature—has gone on before the poems start. The opening of the *Essay on Man* seems by comparison rather formal and hortatory. To be sure, the talk with Bolingbroke prepares for the considerably *more* formal modes of address Pope adopts in the main body of the poem; the beginning cannot be so easy as to jar with the later elevation, and Pope mixes the conversational and the formal with some delicacy. But in the *Moral Essays* one feels a surer intimacy with the poet's voice, a confidence that his tone guarantees his serious engagement with his subject.

Conversational ease is of course more than a matter of beginnings. Throughout the four Epistles the speaking voice moves swiftly and surely through all the ranges of tone from high dignity to the racy indelicacy of a gentleman at ease among gentlemen.[1] The famous passage on the death of the Duke of Buckingham shows this speaking art at work:

> In the worst inn's worst room, with mat half-hung,
> The floors of plaister, and the walls of dung,
> On once a flock-bed, but repair'd with straw,
> With tape-ty'd curtains, never meant to draw,
> The George and Garter dangling from that bed
> Where tawdry yellow strove with dirty red,
> Great Villiers lies—alas! how chang'd from him,
> That life of pleasure, and that soul of whim!
>
> (*Bathurst*, 299–306)

The speaker is at first a kind of camera, ranging about the room and registering visual details with (apparently) a Defoe-like disregard for any principle of selection; when the scene is drawn, he drops his first pose to become a classical elegist mourning the death of a hero. Neither pose, of course, is to be trusted. The description first of all establishes a visual irony, the comment upon Buckingham's career implicit in the contrast between the Garter, the rich emblem of his former glory, and the dinginess of the alehouse in which legend located his death. This irony is echoed in the clash between the harsh consonants and abrupt rhythms of the description and the elegiac dignity and ease of "alas! how chang'd from him." And the apparently random piling up of details builds suspense; we become more and more impatient to find out who is in the room, and the release in the last couplet intensifies the ironic effect of the Virgilian and Miltonic echoes in "how chang'd from him." The variety of tones, the strain of the suspended syntax, the clash of associations evoked by allusion, all these formal oppositions express a moral meaning that is itself complex—one who lives must die, and a life of wealth and pleasure, however amiable, not only cannot fend off death but may indeed make it seem even more shocking than usual. As "moral meaning" this seems flat, but the verse presents it as experience, our experience of following the movement of poetic speech.

The *Moral Essays,* when compared with the *Essay on Man,* show Pope achieving a finer and firmer moral authority in his verse. We trust this speaker not because he tells us to but because we recognize in the easy cultivation of his manner an intelligence about the part discourse plays in human relations—an intelligence we admire and would like to think we share. He can range from eloquence to something close to vulgarity without compromising the Augustan urbanity of his manner. But within that urbanity there are signs of some uncertainty about the Augustan synthesis.

Money and Madness

Three of the *Moral Essays,* the epistles to Cobham, Bathurst, and Burlington, fit conveniently together as a connected exploration of human compulsions and their relation to natural reality. The *Epistle to Cobham* ("Of the Knowledge and Characters of Men") was placed first by Pope in his final arrangement of the series; and its progression, from a rather labored, theoretical treatment of the difficulties of analyzing human character to the wonderfully particular and moving portraits of folly at the end, provides a bridge from the *Essay on Man* to the richer poetic world of the *Moral*

Essays and the Horatian satires. We may pass over the main body of *Cobham,* in which Pope develops the theory of the "ruling passion" as a way of accounting for the apparent chaos of human behavior, and consider the last part of the poem. The keynote is struck in the long examination of Wharton, "the scorn and wonder of our days," whose ruling passion, "the Lust of Praise," destroyed his human identity by destroying his ability to discriminate between experiences:

> Tho' wond'ring Senates hung on all he spoke,
> The Club must hail him master of the joke. . . .
> Then turns repentant, and his God adores
> With the same spirit that he drinks and whores.
>
> (*Cobham,* 184–189)

"Grown all to all," he has in effect become nothing, for he has lost all connection with the world from which he demanded admiration. This is the death of love (201–202), the isolation of the ego in a world of its own making; [2] in short, Wharton is mad in every way that matters.

This alienation of the mind by an unhealthy ruling passion, by a bitter joke of "honest Nature," is the only fact of human life that does not weaken with age: "Time, that on all things lays his lenient hand, / Yet tames not this; it sticks to our last sand" (224–226). The portraits that conclude the poem prove the durability of such madness. The first describes a "rev'rend sire" whom senility and bodily indignity cannot keep from crawling to his mistress; the rest are variations on this same compulsive indifference to decay and imminent death. Helluo the glutton is in love not with jowls of salmon but with the *idea* of eating, just as Euclio cares more about "ownership" than real estate: " 'The Manor! hold,' he cry'd, / 'Not that, I cannot part with that'—and dy'd." Their common malady is that a passion for real experiences has degenerated into abstract obsessions. As they withdraw from solid actuality into the dream-world of their passionate fancies, life dwindles into a fiction of images wholly divorced from the reality they should represent.

This tragic alienation from things as they are is Pope's major theme in the *Moral Essays*. The terms of this theme, as they are to be worked out in the *Epistle to Bathurst*, are outlined in a passage in *Cobham* which Dr. Johnson cherished:

> Court-virtues bear, like Gems, the highest rate,
> Born where Heav'n's influence scarce can penetrate:
> In life's low vale, the soil the virtues like,
> They please as Beauties, here as Wonders strike.
> Tho' the same Sun with all-diffusive rays
> Blush in the Rose, and in the Diamond blaze,
> We prize the stronger effort of his pow'r,
> And justly set the Gem above the Flow'r.
>
> (93–100)

The ironic play is between the "pastoral" attitude that flowers are better than the baubles of urban sophistication and the "commercial" attitude that gems are better than flowers because they are rarer. The "vulgar error that precious stones and metals are created by the sun's rays" [3] allows Pope to say that gems and court-virtues are remarkable things, in fact almost miraculous, at the same time that he calls courts bad places where "Heav'n's influence" (Christian virtues, the *real* ones) has almost no power. In "life's low vale" the virtues grow naturally, because they like the soil; we may pretend to think that court-virtues, like gems, are produced by Heaven's influence too, but we really know that they are unnatural and less admirable than the real thing. "Justly" appeals to a false standard of value, one which measures moral worth by an amoral scale; the social hierarchy, insofar as it is determined by accidents of birth or economics, has no place in the estimation of "character."

This opposition of pastoral and commercial values foreshadows the *Epistle to Bathurst,* where Pope develops his treatment of folly as an alienation from reality into a myth of a pastoral-like harmony between man and nature that rebukes the mores of a money culture.[4] As its alternative title, "Of the Use of Riches," indicates, *Bathurst* examines the effects of wealth upon the society that possesses it, and in particular the relation between prosperity and moral worth. The problem was of course an old one, which by Pope's time had been firmly set in a Protestant context:

> Both fairly owning, Riches in effect
> No grace of Heav'n or Token of th' Elect;
> Giv'n to the Fool, the Mad, the Vain, the Evil,
> To Ward, to Waters, Chartres, and the Devil.
>
> (17–20)

The names are significant: John Ward was a forger, swindler, and financial manipulator, while both Chartres the rake and Peter Walter the scrivener were notorious usurers. Confronted by an infamous alliance of Whiggery, Enterprise Capitalism, and Puritan Dissent, Pope indignantly rejects the Calvinist doctrine that worldly success is a sign of Election, undercutting the sonorous vocabulary of Protestant economic theory with the blunt language of common moral sense, which calls a fool a fool.

A major aim in *Bathurst* is to expose the growing confusion between worldly wealth and moral value, a confusion which R. H. Tawney has scathingly described as it existed at the end of the seventeenth century:

> Not sufficiency to the needs of daily life, but limitless increase and expansion, became the goal of the Christian's efforts. . . . Not an easygoing and open-handed charity, but a systematic and me-

> thodical accumulation, won the meed of praise that belongs to the good and faithful servant. The shrewd, calculating commercialism which tries all human relations by pecuniary standards . . . had evoked from time immemorial the warnings and denunciations of saints and sages. Plunged in the cleansing waters of later Puritanism, the qualities which less enlightened ages had denounced as social vices emerged as economic virtues. They emerged as moral virtues as well. For the world exists not to be enjoyed, but to be conquered.[5]

Though Tawney's ironies sound very much like parts of *Bathurst*, Pope is no Fabian; his position is not radical but ultraconservative, appealing to an aristocratic ethic, firmly rooted in classical and medieval traditions of conduct, which by the 1730's had become obsolete except as a literary ideal. From the time of Horace the "bourgeois" money-maker had been a stock target for satire; Pope gives new edge to the commonplace satiric complaints by relating them to positive assumptions about real wealth and its intimate connections with nature.

The difference between monetary and moral "value" is developed from the opening conversation between Pope and Lord Bathurst.[6] Pope's point is that money and the moral chaos it produces are unnatural, products not of divine design (as Bathurst rather cynically suggests) but of human audacity. Neither squandering nor hoarding money is "right," but "careful Heav'n" had a purpose in creating both misers and spendthrifts, whose actions, in the larger view, ironically preserve the natural balance they individually seem to disturb. But this soothing economic platitude does not appease Pope's sense of the appalling effects of money on individual men. Gold is dangerous because it lacks moral identity (29–34). It reflects perfectly the motives of its users while remaining indifferent as to whether it serves life or death, crime or social good. Though riches can contribute simple necessities— "Meat, Fire, and Cloaths" (82)—even such modest benefits are more than most rich people obtain from their wealth: neither Wharton the prodigal nor Turner the miser received even the simplest pleasures from their fortunes, so engrossed were they in adding to them or getting rid of them (84–86). Like the sad lunatics pictured at the end of *Cobham,* they have abdicated from life to pursue an *idée fixe* with the fervor of the religious ascetic. And beyond common necessities, riches are useless: "What can they give? to dying Hopkins Heirs; / To Chartres, Vigour; Japhet, Nose and Ears?" "Material" wealth is an abstraction, with no power over physical experience. Rich people, as Hemingway tried to tell Fitzgerald, can be as miserable as anyone else. It would be sentimental to suppose that riches themselves create unhappiness; wealth obviously can command gratifications beyond the dreams of the poor. But wealth comes from devoting to monetary symbols the kind of loving attention one might otherwise devote to people and things; and symbols, Pope knows, have a way of overpowering immediate human pleasures. Harpax could have bought himself friendship of a sort, "were Harpax not too wise to spend" (93)—economic "wisdom" is only a neurotic version of what common sense calls madness.

The destruction of pleasure, however, is less serious than the destruction of charity and social love that riches also cause. In lines 101–108 Pope runs through a catalogue of attitudes toward the poor. There is Denis Bond, the Charitable Corporation swindler, who is at least honest about his brutality— "Bond damns the Poor, and hates them from his heart." Sir Gilbert Heathcote simply abides by his business axiom that "every man in want is knave or fool." Sir John Blunt, in the Calvinist way, equals his success and other men's failures to God's providence and "piously denies" charity. Only the "good

Bishop" admits that financial failure need not deprive a man of Grace—but since God may be trusted to love the poor, he himself need not bother. (Warburton's insistence that this bishop is imaginary makes Pope's swipe at Anglican Indifferentism even more damning—presumably *many* bishops would fit the case.) Moral rectitude is no substitute for love, especially when it is a rectitude founded upon economic success. Almost all the people Pope attacks in *Bathurst* have roughly the same relation to riches; few inherited their wealth, as did Bathurst, the large majority being self-made successes. And a catalogue of their activities is revealing: *Usurers:* Chartres, Peter Walter, Turner, Hopkins, Blunt; *Swindlers:* Ward, Chartres, Crook, Bond, Sutton, Blunt; *Projectors and Stock-Market Plungers:* Bond, Blunt, Gage, Sutton, Cutler; *Misers:* Selkirk, Hopkins, Heathcote, Cutler, Wortley Montagu; *Speculators and Prodigals:* Wharton, "Phryne," Villiers, Colepepper, "Uxorio." Their common ground (except for the prodigals, who work in reverse) is the attempt to create wealth out of nothing, to divorce riches by a kind of economic alchemy from the nature that is the source of all real value. Pope's poetic role in *Bathurst* is the serious critic of the moral disturbances that accompanied finance capitalism's imposition of its values upon a society that was, historically and imaginatively, agrarian and Christian. English capitalism was well established as early as the sixteenth century, and as L. C. Knights has shown, one of the main concerns of the Jacobean dramatists was the clash between traditional norms of conduct and the new morality of self-aggrandizement and impersonality that was felt to characterize the man of business in his assault on the old social order.[7] By Pope's time the battle was all but over; *Bathurst* was written after the South-Sea bubble had burst and the malpractices of the Charitable Corporation had become common scandal. Pope himself suffered losses in the South-Sea fiasco, and his bitterness is not wholly disinterested. But the poem takes a larger view of the cycle of boom and bust—it is only one symptom of an appalling economic and moral revolution.

The instruments of this revolution, the usurers and projectors, lack social love because of a misapprehension about nature. They imagine (113–124) a future of dearth which blinds them to the importance of present gratification, either for themselves or others. Their knowledge of economic arcana blurs the fact that money is humanly meaningful only when it purchases substantial commodities. They seem to mistrust nature's ability to reproduce goods, and in their anxiety to corner the market in bread or men they forget that the supply ultimately depends not on price indexes but on the permanent rhythms of growth and death. Like religious fanatics they pursue "some Revelation hid from you and me," an inner light that seems lunatic to common sense; and they have the fanatic's indifference to the existence of other people's views and feelings.

Nature and Abstraction

Pope can attack these delusions because he sees beyond them to a vision of natural richness and regularity that shows up the abstract meanness of commercial amorality.[8] The vision is embodied in the verse itself, first of all, in the way literary allusion figures as moral commentary; classical and biblical echoes evoke a past whose values were clearer and firmer. Buckingham's deathbed, "where tawdry yellow strove with dirty red," is measured against another occasion of death, the funeral games for Anchises where Cloanthus' victory was rewarded with a mantle "where gold and purple strive in equal rows" (Dryden's *Aeneid,* V, 326). Allusion underscores the vulgarity and abstractness of the present with reminders that life was not always so. But even in the present, nature is available as a measure of goodness. Bribery, for example, is the product of money and not of natural goods (35–78), and it can be ridiculed by imagining the embarrassments of bribing people with substantial things. Even gold is awkward sometimes, since it has physical reality, but human ingenuity has completed the process of abstraction by inventing "blest paper-credit," which "lends Corruption lighter wings to fly." *Bathurst* chronicles the perversion of nature by wealth, but nature remains imaginatively available as a measure of that perversion.

This measure is fully revealed in the great passage about extremes working toward an ultimate synthesis in goodness:

> "Extremes in Nature equal good produce,
> "Extremes in Man concur to gen'ral use."
> Ask we what makes one keep, and one bestow?
> That Pow'r who bids the Ocean ebb and flow,
> Bids seed-time, harvest, equal course maintain,
> Thro' reconcil'd extremes of drought and rain,
> Builds Life on Death, on Change Duration founds,
> And gives th' eternal wheels to know their rounds. (163–170)

The lines evoke the great rhythms of nature that a concern merely for artificial wealth may obscure, and they reassure us that nature is finally too powerful to be overcome by human abstractions. As usual, the reassurance is far from naïve; the great natural fact is change, and the power of false wealth to destroy man's awareness of change cannot be taken lightly. Like all madmen, the financiers are in some ways happier than the rest of us, for their lives are abstract and simple, relieved of physical labor and the painful sense of complexity that characterizes sane intelligence. Finally, however, Pope chooses sanity, for though the sane man who consoles himself with the imaginative vision of permanence in change may be no more "happy" than the madman who consoles himself with his own fantasies, still sanity is at least not lonely—its activities take place in a community of understanding and agreement formed of all right-thinking men, living and dead. The financiers must dwell alone in private worlds of their own hallucinations, and their tragic rejection of community predicts an ominous future.

In the "reconcil'd extremes" passage Pope brings to imaginative life one of the key doctrines of the *Essay on Man* (see Epistle II, 203–216), giving it a solidity of meaning that the more theoretical context of the Essay cannot fully provide. This passage is the axis, so to speak, of *Bathurst,* the moral center about which the details of the poem are organized.[9] Its implications sum up and judge the lack of faith in nature that marks the folly and wickedness of the financiers. Its high Biblical tone, for example, contrasts sharply with the ironic interplay of verbal elevation and meanness in the prophecy that accounts for Blunt's avarice (137–140). Blunt, not understanding that nature is regular and immutable, believes that money is the only firm agency of order. But Pope sees further; his view takes in the natural rhythms that can usefully assimilate even folly, and the vision of "reconcil'd extremes" emphasizes the positive attitudes toward wealth that have begun to control the poem. Even misers and money-grubbers, considered in this broad perspective, turn out to be contributors to order, "backward steward[s] for the poor":

> This year a Reservoir, to keep and spare,
> The next a Fountain, spouting thro' his Heir,
> In lavish streams to quench a Country's thirst,
> And men and dogs shall drink him 'till they
> burst. (175–178)

The images are significant: the financier does not become good until he can be seen not as a human being but as a natural force, or the conduit through which such force can run. Nature can adapt into its own scheme even money and the wretched social indifference it breeds; the wealth that "pale Mammon" amassed so scrupulously is sardonically revealed as the fountainhead from which pours an indiscriminate flood of refreshment, for beasts as well as men.

But the reconciliation of extremes is no placid metaphor for perfection of economic process. Line 178 couples "men and *dogs*," a fairly blunt indication of the unreasoning, self-destructive greed through which the righting of the balance operates. Pope takes long views and short ones at the same time—here he is both pleased by the way redistribution completes a natural cycle and regretful about the human frailty that starts the next cycle even as it completes the last one. This double view figures also in the treatment of Cotta the miser and his prodigal son. Cotta's mania for accumulation destroyed the proper intimacy and geniality of the agrarian life— "No rafter'd roofs with dance and tabor sound, / No noontide-bell invites the country round" (191–192)—but he is no worse than his son, who mistakes "reverse of wrong for right" and dispenses "slaughter'd hecatombs" and "floods of wine" to all and sundry. The father ruined the traditional tone of the natural life, but the son goes so far in the opposite direction as to destroy its tangible being, selling his forests, his livestock, and finally the land itself "for his Country's love" —which may mean that he loves his country but more likely that he wants it to love him. Balance is temporarily restored, but only through a sad revelation of vanity.

Scrutiny of economic process thus reveals the operation of a cycle, one comfortingly analogous to natural rhythms and yet disturbingly dependent upon human folly. Mandeville, a less humane commentator on the process, could merely observe the facts and laugh in the faces of his self-righteous readers. But Pope characteristically seeks a way of reconciling the cycle with the human potential for goodness. He does so by resorting to the myth of pastoral—a myth that, as we shall see, he raises to its highest possible pitch of affirmation at the end of the *Epistle to Burlington.*

In *Bathurst,* as shown in the story of Cotta's son (213–218), the pastoral motive centers around the fall from grace, the loss of a golden age of country innocence. The Man of Ross, Pope's exemplar of the proper use of riches, shows how pastoral feelings are enlisted in the service of the social thesis. He is a kind of superman of the Christian virtues, who feeds the poor and aged, portions maidens and apprentices orphans, heals the sick and administers justice. But his achievements are not wholly in the realm of "fact":

> Who hung with woods yon mountain's sultry
>   brow?
> From the dry rock who bid the waters
>   flow? . . .
> Who taught that heav'n-directed spire to rise?
> The MAN of Ross, each lisping babe replies.
> (253–262)

The details are drawn from the real John Kyrle's patronage of landscape gardening and civil engineering, but the effect is more than factual. He is projected almost as a pastoral magician, whose intentions are realized by nature without the intervention of physical agency. The "invocation" is pastoral commonplace:

> Rise, honest Muse! and sing the MAN of Ross:
> Pleas'd Vaga echoes thro' her winding bounds,
> And rapid Severn hoarse applause resounds.
> (250–252)

This nature reflects country realities—the muse is "honest" and the applause "hoarse." Pope's enthusiasm is far from innocent. But the pastoral framing of the Man of Ross, for all its qualifications, points to a natural reinforcement of human motives that we are to take very seriously. He exemplifies the conscious use of riches to sustain and enrich nature and the society based on nature. He re-enacts, with his dependents and with the landscape, the loving dealings of God with nature and of Christ with man. His exercise of love strips away superfluous social abstractions— "Despairing Quacks with curses fled the place, / And vile Attornies, now an useless race"—and restores to human relations their "original" simplicity and warmth. (We are to recall who it was that drove the money-changers from the temple.) He thus stands as a living rebuke to a loveless financier like Cutler, who "saw tenants break, and houses fall" and "his only daughter in a stranger's pow'r" (323–326) because his mania had persuaded him that he could not afford to build a wall or pay a dower, thus sacrificing relations with people for an empty symbol.

But the Man of Ross does not conclude *Bathurst*. Pope reserves that place for the tale of Sir Balaam—the natural measure gets no triumphant realization, but rather it remains as a potent but distant possibility. Unlike the Man of Ross, Sir Balaam lives in the city—in fact in the City, the inner stronghold of urban commercial attitudes—and *his* "sober fame" is the façade of bourgeois respectability. His are the Puritan virtues in apotheosis, compounded of self-denial, mechanical piety, and economic solidity. This is moral vacuity and not vice, Pope sees, but nature abhors a vacuum; Balaam's career is the saga of the creation of evil *ex nihilo*. If "virtue" is only a restraint and not a positive impulse, it is helpless in the face of worldly temptation, and Balaam's financial success brings disaster: "What late he call'd a Blessing, now was Wit, / And God's good Providence, a lucky Hit." Pope has his eye on the transition from bourgeois entrepreneur to would-be aristocrat, the peculiar twilight zone in which things (and men) indeed "change their titles, as our manners turn." This out-of-focus Rake's Progress moves swiftly to its conclusion as Balaam remarries a "Nymph of Quality," bows at court, endures the moral and physical destruction of his family, and is finally himself executed for financially motivated treason:

Wife, son, and daughter, Satan, are thy own,
His wealth, yet dearer, forfeit to the Crown,
The Devil and the King divide the prize,
And sad Sir Balaam curses God and dies.

(399–402)

This modern Job, tempted, as Pope says, by a Satan who has learned that wealth is a more efficient corrupter than poverty, perishes in desolation of both spirit and substance, the spirit and substance he has so hopelessly confounded.

The simple manner of narration does not obscure the tale's masterful relevance to the poem's major theme. Pope makes no sentimental claim that this is a good man gone wrong, but there still is a certain pathos in seeing a not particularly bad man destroyed because he is too stupid to resist or even recognize money's power to excite all his worst impulses. Taken as a summary of all the usurers' and projectors' maladies, Balaam shows that Pope's ideas about the abuse of riches are not the moral clichés we are so accustomed to hear. Balaam is not exactly "selfish," for example, since nothing suggests that he pursues money to gratify any substantial desires of his own. The extra pudding he eats is not an object of his activity but a sign of its success—his wife thinks conspicuous consumption is appropriate to their new dignity, and so they consume. He remarries not because he desires the Nymph of Quality but because she desires him (or more probably his money), and he becomes a courtier not to satisfy his own vanity but "to please the fair." In fact, there is no object to his pursuit of wealth save the pursuit itself; and his amiable mindlessness may be even more contemptible than honest greed. The other financiers in one way or another show this same lack of concern for self, as it is ordinarily thought of. Shylock starves himself, Mammon "pine[s] amidst his store," Cotta "liv'd on pulse," Cutler banishes the doctor from his deathbed. Most of the others deny themselves pleasure or even comfort for the sake of their obsessions; though some are selfish in motive, none draw from their activities any substantial benefit to the self. As Max Weber observed:

> The ideal type of the capitalistic entrepreneur . . . avoids ostentation and unnecessary expenditure, as well as conscious enjoyment of his power. . . . His manner of life is, in other words, often . . . distinguished by a certain ascetic tendency. . . . He gets nothing out of his wealth for himself, except the irrational sense of having done his job well.[10]

"Materialism," too, is an inadequate label for the state of mind Pope attacks in *Bathurst*. As such satirists as Veblen and Kenneth Burke have mordantly demonstrated, whatever a capitalistic society is interested in, it is not much interested in material *things*. Mr. Burke's description of the finance capitalist is remarkably close to Pope's:

> No poet was ever so delicate and fanciful in his conception of the realities as those dreamers, those men of vision. . . . Here the superstructure of credit and interest is considered basic, quite as though one were to think of a transfer of goods as *incidental* and were to find soundness only in the paper on which the transaction was recorded. . . . A railroad is approached, not in terms of tracks, engines, roundhouses, repair plants, and working force, but through data as to its capital structure![11]

This is not materialism, as Pope sees, but a kind of mad spirituality. He is in fact an advocate *for* a traditional materialism of a limited sort. In *Bathurst* he expresses a view of secular wealth that is precisely that of St. Thomas: "It is lawful to desire temporal blessings, not putting them in the first place, as though setting up our rest in them, but regarding them as aids to blessedness, inasmuch as they support our corporal life and serve as instruments for acts of virtue."[12] The realms of matter and spirit, though related, are to be kept distinct, and each has rights of its own; when this distinction breaks down and the material is spiritualized, the sin of Avarice results.

The Epistle itself is of course not so openly doctrinal. Pope's feelings are "rendered" in a swift progression of scenes and portraits of folly and misconduct—the moral commentary emerges from particular details of dramatized human behavior. But behind the drama we recognize a firmly defined moral vocabulary, one that incorporates both classical and Christian ethical terms. The imagery often suggests that the financiers are sinning not against dogma but against nature itself; their abstract approach to experience is wrong because it in effect denies the potent myth of a beautiful and harmonious relationship between man and his environment—the relationship, between a fruitful, regular nature and the human creatures who assist and use it, so movingly reasserted in Pound's *Canto LI:*

> With usury has no man a good house
> made of stone, no paradise on his church wall
> With usury the stone cutter is kept from his
> stone
> the weaver is kept from his loom by usura
> Wool does not come into market
> the peasant does not eat his own grain
> . . . .
> Usury kills the child in the womb
> And breaks short the young man's courting
> Usury brings age into youth; it lies between
> the bride
> and the bridegroom
> Usury is against Nature's increase.

The Triumph of Sense

The *Epistle to Burlington,* though the first of the *Moral Essays* in date of composition, was placed by Pope last in his roughly thematic rearrangement of the four poems, and it brilliantly defines the end toward which the poems are pointed. It is in effect the major chord upon which the *Moral Essays* end, as a satiric attack on tasteless prodigality leads to an Augustan vision of man and nature in harmonious agreement.

As a counterpart to *Bathurst, Burlington* examines not the accumulation of riches but the squandering of them; but Pope finds a psychological affinity between the two activities. Where the miser endeavors "to gain those Riches he can ne'er enjoy," the prodigal labors "to purchase what he ne'er can taste" (1–4). Neither, in short, is in substantial contact with his wealth, and both violate natural order. Still Timon, Pope's exemplar of prodigality, calls for somewhat different treatment from that accorded the villains in *Bathurst:*

> Who but must laugh, the Master when he sees,
> A puny insect, shiv'ring at a breeze!
>
> (*Burlington,* 107–108)

> My Lord advances with majestic mien,
> Smit with the mighty pleasure, to be seen.
>
> (127–128)

> Treated, caress'd, and tir'd, I take my leave,
> Sick of his civil Pride from Morn to Eve.
>
> (165–166)

The effect is a general diminishment of the object, and while the feeling ranges from irritation to contempt, a certain amusement replaces the moral outrage so common in *Bathurst:*

> When Hopkins dies, a thousand lights attend
> The wretch, who living sav'd a candle's end:
> Should'ring God's altar a vile image stands,
> Belies his features, nay extends his hands.
>
> (*Bathurst,* 291–294)

This magnification is hardly amusing; we may smile sympathetically at Pope's fretful rejection of Timon's civil pride, but we must be indignant about Hopkins, who is *evil* in the sacrilegious vulgarity of his funeral service and monument. One may pity Timon, who after all suffers from his own lack of taste almost as much as do his guests, even though he does not understand that it is suffering; but in *Bathurst* we are not often asked to pity anyone.

This is not to say that Pope treats bad taste lightly. Timon, like the financiers, violates natural principles which we are to take very seriously indeed. Still, Timon's folly is not in reducing natural substance to items on business indexes and deposit slips, but rather in contriving particular, substantial things that unfortunately distort the ideals of reality. He half-recognizes nature, as the financiers do not, but his understanding is too feeble for him to imitate nature in a meaningful creative act. Creative participation in reality is finally futile unless conducted with intelligent care for the forms and procedures that nature seems to prescribe. Timon is especially irritating because he comes close to doing the right thing; only one ingredient, "taste," is lacking, and the poem describes the effects of this lack and criticizes them by a comparison to the achievements of true taste, past and present.

The opening lines, with their comment on the prodigal's extravagant pursuit of "what he ne'er can taste," introduce a major theme. The prodigal creates *discomfort* for himself and others by his inhuman carelessness about pleasure. He "sees, or hears, or eats" on the advice of experts (5–12), and his purchased experiences really gratify him "no more / Than his fine Wife, alas! or finer Whore." The ambiguity of "taste" is important; "physical" and "esthetic" are the same to the prodigal, because he has no firsthand experience of either. This blurring of distinctions culminates in the play on "fine." Pretending to adopt the prodigal's own point of view, Pope calls the wife "fine," apparently in the sense of "good, well bred, personally admirable in various ways." "Alas" thus seems at first a sign of sincere regret ("the fool doesn't appreciate such a fine woman"), but "finer Whore" gives the joke away: the wife is a "fine lady," stylish and well kept, but she's eclipsed by the more stylish and even better-kept mistress, and "alas" becomes a mocking comment on the fact that this man's women have been purchased for the esthetic or physical enjoyment of others, like the statues and "dirty Gods."

The prodigal, by buying more than he can understand or enjoy, becomes a connoisseur of discomfort. He and his kind are "Conscious they act a true Palladian part, / And, if they starve, they starve by rules of art" (37–38). The cultivated life becomes a kind of playacting as they dramatize themselves and their deeds with ludicrous self-importance, without reflecting that the finest art has roots in life. Behind the poem lies a pun on "imitation" that contrasts the true classical mimesis with the slavish copying, not of nature, but of other works of art. Timon and his friends imitate Burlington's imitation of Palladio's imitation of classical architecture; but where Burlington understands the reasons behind the designs, their combination of beauty and use, his imitators are concerned only with forms abstracted from practical considerations. The perverse asceticism of discomfort as a way of life is fully revealed at Timon's villa. Timon is surrounded by gargantuan magnificence—"his building is a Town, / His pond an Ocean"—and the effect is to dwarf the owner himself, who in this monstrous perspective ceases to seem human: "A puny insect, shiv'ring at a breeze!" His decorative lake serves only to accentuate "the keenness of the Northern wind"; his summerhouse "knows no shade"; one must "thro' the length of yon hot Terrace sweat" and climb "ten steep slopes" to approach his villa; and at his dinner table the pleasures of the board are nullified by the mechanical regularity of the service— "In plenty starving, tantaliz'd in state." The only comfort to be found in this establishment, ironically, is in the sybaritic chapel: "To rest, the Cushion and soft Dean invite, / Who never mentions Hell to ears polite." In contrast, the dining room, which *ought* to be devoted to ease and pleasure, is the scene of something very like a religious ceremony:

> Is this a dinner? this a Genial room?
> No, 'tis a Temple, and a Hecatomb.
> A solemn Sacrifice, perform'd in state.
> (155–157)

Experience is all out of kilter in this grotesque temple of bad taste, where even the dinners taste bad. Feelings get divorced from their proper objects and attached to new ones with startling incongruity.

Prodigality, through its violation of proper principles of behavior, is an offense against man and society, but it is also an offense against nature, from which standards of propriety are derived; and it is this second aspect of prodigality that directs the development of *Burlington* into the powerful climax of the *Moral Essays*. The development runs from a description of violation, through a consideration of what has been violated, to a positive definition of a noble role for man to play in the life of nature.

The strongest counteragent to prodigality is a quality of mind Pope calls "sense":

> Good Sense, which only is the gift of Heav'n,
> And tho' no science, fairly worth the seven:
> A Light, which in yourself you must perceive,
> Jones and Le Nôtre have it not to give. (43–46)

"Sense" is inherent, an instinct that cannot be cultivated but that is the equal of all the cultivated arts and sciences. Though Pope's use of the term includes our "common sense," practical, pragmatic intelligence, he suggests a further dimension of meaning by comparing it to the religious "inner light." The light of sense, however, is not merely subjective and personal, for it has the power to illuminate and glorify human works: " 'Tis Use alone that sanctifies Expence, / And Splendor borrows all her rays from Sense" (179–180). "Sense" and "Use" are practically synonymous; the personal resource is measured by the social product, and the optimum result is a translation of the economic ("Expence") into the spiritual ("sanctifies"), under the auspices, as we shall see, of a nature that is essentially benevolent. Pope draws also on associations with "sensation" and "sensibility." "Good sense" can mean something like "a clear and sensitive response to natural reality." The good builder or planter must follow nature ("In all, let Nature never be forgot"), and to do so he must apprehend nature sensuously by consulting "the Genius of the Place" (57–64), the real agent of beauty that "paints as you plant, and, as you work, designs." Sense is an inner light, but it alone makes possible the fullest community with external nature; it is a private possession, but Pope could assume that it was the mutual property of the best men in a given culture. We may define it, crudely enough, as the esthetic intelligence of a cultivated society.

By the exercise of sense one becomes an instrument or even a colleague of nature. If you work with an eye to the original harmony of natural things, the Genius of the Place, your own productions will seem a part of nature itself:

> Still follow Sense, of ev'ry Art the Soul,
> Parts answ'ring parts shall slide into a whole,
> Spontaneous beauties all around advance,
> Start ev'n from Difficulty, strike from Chance;
> Nature shall join you, Time shall make it grow
> A Work to wonder at—perhaps a STOW. (65–70)

Here is a practical version of the mythic union of nature and human experience Pope considered in the *Pastorals*. Nature is alive, in a way, but its vitality now seems drawn not from an obedient reflection of human feelings but from some inner principle of organization. Man finds a relation with the natural world not by ascribing his own emotions to it but by "sensing" the designs and poises already there and making his own activities consonant with them. This new vision of order defines a poetic speaker who sees time not as an enemy (as in the *Pastorals*) but as a friend. The pastoral shepherd has no society and so must gauge every event in terms of his own limited experience; but when you are in a society, and can see that events may have more significance than your personal experience can unfold—if, in short, you can apprehend nature's designs and cooperate with them —then "Nature shall join you."

But time seems friendly only to the man of sense: "Without it, proud Versailles! thy glory falls; / And Nero's Terraces desert their walls" (71–72). Pope has a double sense of the mutability that pervades the poem. Time, as usual, figures as the relentless enemy of human works—Villario's "ten-years toil" at landscaping ends with his realization that nature can do the job better, and the woods that Sabinus loved are cut down to satisfy his son's "fine Taste" for "an op'ner Vista." This pessimistic view of time is, however, balanced by an emphasis on nature's ability to renew itself ceaselessly. Time may be hostile to human works, but it is the necessary condition of natural growth and fruition— "Time shall make it grow."

> Another age shall see the golden Ear
> Imbrown the Slope, and nod on the Parterre,
> Deep Harvests bury all his pride has plann'd,
> And laughing Ceres re-assume the land.
>
> (173–176)

The "inverted Nature" of Timon's barren estate will eventually be righted through nature's insistence on growth and utility.

In its emphasis on the fertility and permanence of nature, *Burlington* clarifies Pope's attitude toward the criminality of the financiers and the stupidity of Timon. The Earl of Burlington himself appears in the poem as the symbol of intelligence, which understands and respects traditional values and can translate the lessons of the past into meaningful present activity: "You show us, Rome was glorious, not profuse, / And pompous buildings once were things of Use" (23–24). "Glory" and "glorious" are nearly always ironic words in Pope's later poems, and the serious use of "glorious" here is especially powerful. "Glory" combines tangible splendor with utility; the external lineaments of the building express the practical function it exists to serve. This early couplet prepares for the key generalization that " 'Tis Use alone that sanctifies Expence," and architecture becomes a metaphor for the sensible creativity through which man can cooperate with natural process. The metaphor gains force from its conjunction with another kind of human creativity: "Who then shall grace, or who improve the Soil? / Who plants like BATHURST, or who builds like BOYLE" (177–178). Landscape gardening represents creative activity in direct contact with nature, the planned improvement of the world upon the model of natural growth. Timon's garden was a ghastly inversion of nature— "Trees cut to Statues, Statues thick as Trees"—but the finest gardening differs only subtly from nature itself, as Pope had argued in *The Guardian* (No. 173, September 29, 1713) some twenty years earlier. The trick is "decently to hide" the evidences of the gardener's calculation: "He gains all points, who pleasingly confounds, / Surprizes, varies, and conceals the Bounds" (55–56). The bounds exist, for this is a finite imitation of nature rather than the real thing, but the edges of the composition are carefully minimized, unlike Timon's garden, where "On ev'ry side you look, behold the Wall!"

Proper gardening, with its emphasis on natural arrangement and growth, is a kind of farming, or at least it shares with farming the moral dignity Pope associates with the productive cultivation of the soil. The irrepressible natural vigor that will submerge Timon's monstrous creations presents no threat to the "sensible" planter, whose domain appears at the end of *Burlington* as almost an Eden, where traditional possession, amicable relations with neighbors and tenants, and natural richness are sustained by modesty and hard work (181–190). The life of nature and the life of man come together in a harmonious whole as the speaking tone shifts from informal conversation to the balanced cadences of high oratory, which seem almost to reflect the recurrent rhythms of life and growth with which the lines deal. The poem draws to a lofty close with a passage exhorting Burlington to new efforts, so that kings will emulate him in public works that may maintain peace between man and nature:

> Bid the broad Arch the dang'rous Flood contain,
> The Mole projected break the roaring Main;
> Back to his bounds their subject Sea command,
> And roll obedient Rivers thro' the Land;
> These Honours, Peace to happy Britain brings,
> These are Imperial Works, and worthy Kings.
> (199–204)

The pastoral "magic" that controls nature becomes literal fact through the sensible creativity of the Augustan genius.

This vision of useful art is perhaps the most "Augustan" passage Pope ever wrote. Our full appreciation of what it positively asserts depends on our recollection of the alternatives, the kinds of fruitless activity described in the other *Moral Essays*. Pope, that is to say, offers his vision of peaceful order not as cheerful prediction but as intellectual possibility, asserted in defiance of a powerfully realized understanding that the tendency of history was toward quite another state of affairs. For one Bathurst there were twenty Shylocks; Burlington was a remarkable individual, but "A hundred smart in *Timon* and in *Balaam*" (*Sat. II i.* 42). What would seem, out of context, an expression of simple confidence in the power of "good Sense" becomes, through its placement at the end of a series, a courageous refusal to forsake an ideal simply because fact seemed hostile to its fulfillment.

The vision is in fact another of Pope's imaginative visions, firmly based upon the Augustan idea of the Roman tradition, in which art and ordinary experience were fused. It would be wrong to say that the vision was empty because in the eighteenth century England was actually moving toward the opposite of pastoral perfection. Pope knew this as well as we do. The passage expresses the kind of truth that any operative myth will express; we respond not to "fact" but to the intelligent courage that rises above the merely factual to assert imaginatively the permanent possibility of goodness in the human condition. This is one of the greatest moments of English neoclassicism; the spatial and intellectual contraction of the opening of *Cobham,* where the "man to Books confin'd" railed at humanity from his study, has developed into a broad generalization about man and nature that is wholly convincing—convincing because Pope has earned our respect and belief through the honest clarity with which he faces all the difficulties his argument raises.

The Edge of Tragedy

Pope never entirely regained the daylight mood of the *Epistle to Burlington.* The *Imitations of Horace* and the revised *Dunciad* reveal a declension into darker areas of experience as the poise between the actual and the ideal grows harder to sustain. In the 1730's Pope moved from high Augustanism toward a new kind of art, whose structural and expressive principle is not so much balance as exaggeration. Though this new art is visible in the first versions of the *Dunciad* (1728, 1729), I think its relation to the Augustan mode emerges more clearly if one first considers *Of the Characters of Women: an Epistle to a Lady* (1735). Pope placed this magnificent poem second in his final arrangement of the *Moral Es-*

says, but it was written last, and it differs from its companions in important ways. It is built in the Augustan way, by playing off two very dissimilar kinds of feeling: on the surface it is a traditional satiric attack on feminine folly, yet at its climax, the great section on the death of dowagers (219–248), satire yields to something like a tragic view of the effects of time and change that everyone—women and men alike—must someday confront and yield to. The change is marked in the tone: the easy informality of the satiric epistle gives way to the lofty resonances of the orator-preacher as the poem moves out of the limited world of personal abnormality into a realm where "normal" and "abnormal" have no meaning. Pope returns to the social world at the end, to be sure, and brings back with him a new perspective on what a woman should be; but the process of transcendence and return produces an irony that delicately qualifies the beautiful tribute to Martha Blount. The element of "tragedy" must not be overstressed; its power stems from the contrast with the satiric parts, and our sense of the poem as dramatic interplay and redefinition would vanish if either element were to crowd out the other. Such "tragic" feelings, however, become increasingly strong in Pope's later works. Although *To a Lady* keeps the opposing elements—positive social perspective and sorrowful understanding of time's indifference—in equilibrium, the equilibrium becomes more and more difficult to sustain.

The opening address to his dedicatee sets a tone of teasing mock-wonder at female inconsistency that persists in the earlier satiric portraits—judicious Silia flies into a tantrum over a pimple on her nose, while Papillia yearns for a park only to find she can't endure trees. But as the poem proceeds, inconsistency seems more disturbing. Narcissa, Philomedé, Flavia, and Atossa are all in some way actresses, compulsively theatricalizing life instead of living it. Like the tragic fools at the end of *Cobham,* they enact their inner fantasies as though they were experiences. Whether they feel too little, like Chloe, or too much, like Atossa, they are isolated from every reality except death. Death in fact hovers around them; it has in store for these changeable creatures the greatest change of all, and it dominates the climax of the poem, the passage on "the fate of a whole Sex of Queens." The teasing satirist assumes a graver voice ("Yet mark the fate") which is not just addressing Martha Blount as it traces the restless progress of aging charmers:

> Beauties, like Tyrants, old and friendless grown,
> Yet hate Repose, and dread to be alone,
> Worn out in public, weary ev'ry eye,
> Nor leave one sigh behind them when they die. (*To a Lady*, 227–230)

The view is a mixed one. Pope finds them foolish, but there is something heroic in their hopeless battle and something callous in the world's indifference.

At the climax of the poem Pope squarely confronts both the moral childishness and the pathos of these women:

> At last, to follies Youth could scarce defend,
> It grows their Age's prudence to pretend;
> Asham'd to own they gave delight before,
> Reduc'd to feign it, when they give no more:
> As Hags hold Sabbaths, less for joy then spight,
> So these their merry, miserable Night;
> Still round and round the Ghosts of Beauty glide,
> And haunt the places where their Honour dy'd. (235–242)

Mr. Empson remarks on the passage:

> What is so compelling is the combination within it of two sharply distinguished states of mind; the finicking precision with which the subject-matter is handled; the pity, bitterness, and terror with which the subject-matter must be conceived. . . .

> Pope finds himself indeed hag-ridden by these poor creatures; they excite in him feelings irrelevantly powerful, of waste, of unavoidable futility, which no bullying of [the] object can satisfy.[13]

This emphasis on doubleness is important. Pope is exposing the spiritual hollowness that lurks behind vanity, the shocking self-mystification of defining "prudence" as a deliberate pretense of wickedness, and the abysmal emotional emptiness that conceals love when it exists and feigns it when it doesn't. As women, they are beneath contempt. But as human beings, these ghosts of beauty have a more complex claim upon our feelings; for all their folly, they show the operation of a fundamental human impulse.

This impulse is the human need to resist change. Women are inconstant and unprincipled, Pope has said, but at the climax of *To a Lady* he comes to see them in a new light. They *have* a kind of character, in their pathetically stubborn "rage to live," to maintain personality with all its defects against the attack of time. Their resistance of course fails—

> See how the World its Veterans rewards!
> A Youth of frolicks, an old Age of Cards,
> Fair to no purpose, artful to no end,
> Young without Lovers, old without a Friend,
> A Fop their Passion, but their Prize a Sot,
> Alive, ridiculous, and dead, forgot! (243–248)

—but a pitiful dignity invests their feeble efforts to keep their identities. They remain women, but they have come to represent a predicament all human beings share. And although their way of coping with their predicament is badly flawed—there are better ways to die—still the ways that good, sensible people choose are in the long run no more effective, in the light of cold fact. As usual, however, Pope will not settle for cold fact. Having brought the poem close to tragedy, he retreats into Augustan common sense. Death is inevitable, but some kinds of aging and dying are more admirable than others. This shift is marked by the return of the personal tone:

> Ah Friend! to dazzle let the Vain design,
> To raise the Thought and touch the Heart, be thine!
> That Charm shall grow, while what fatigues the Ring
> Flaunts and goes down, an unregarded thing.
> So when the Sun's broad beam has tir'd the sight,
> All mild ascends the Moon's more sober light,
> Serene in Virgin Modesty she shines,
> And unobserv'd the glaring Orb declines.
>
> (249–256)

This lovely compliment carries an unobtrusive irony: "Your inner beauty is more lasting and pleasing than the outer beauty of foolish women, and it will eventually outshine theirs, but you won't triumph until you, like them, are old." But the image of the moon, even though it may faintly echo Pope's earlier resolution to "Catch, ere she change, the Cynthia of this minute" (20) and so qualify delicately the compliment, mainly asserts his admiration for Miss Blount's spiritual beauty.

The end of *To a Lady* distances, though it does not dismiss, the tragic problem of death. Pope has faced it squarely at the climax, the most impressive and memorable part of the poem, and the end represents the kind of withdrawal from tragic fact that is necessary for the maintenance of life, or at least of sanity. Again the recourse is to myth, in this case a myth that opposes to time and death a loving personal relationship. But in comparison to the *Epistle to Burlington*, whose conclusion constructed myth from the materials of some two thousand years of ethical and esthetic tradition, the withdrawal into personal relations at the end of *To a Lady* seems tenuously private. The power with which the vision of human futility has been stated brings the poem closer to tragedy than any of the other *Moral*

Essays; To a Lady seems on the verge of breaking the pattern of meaning Pope develops in *Cobham, Bathurst,* and *Burlington*—the affirmation that a loving natural relationship can exist between man and his world. It lingers ominously on the possibility that the positive potential of experience is gravely limited. Pope ends by minimizing this possibility, and the interaction between satiric and tragic feeling leads to a poetic triumph that remains Augustan; but as the gap between moments of tragic perception and positive general attitudes widens, it seems as though Pope is moving toward a new kind of poetic structure and subject matter.

Still, *To a Lady* has its place in the *Moral Essays,* which (it should be insisted) need to be read as a whole. The set of poems stands with *Songs of Experience, Middlemarch,* and the novels of D. H. Lawrence as one of the most profound expressions in English literature of how the psychic disorders of the inner life subvert our relations with people and things, with that world of "substance" that is the primary condition of our humanity. As George Eliot puts it in *Middlemarch:* "There is no general doctrine which is not capable of eating out our morality if unchecked by the deep-seated habit of direct fellow-feeling with individual fellow-men." The *Moral Essays,* to be sure, show something less than George Eliot's all-embracing pity for men and women who unknowingly try to adjust reality to suit their faulty imaginations, just as Pope's tone expresses something less than Blake's or Lawrence's vatic indignation about doctrinal violations of substance. His Augustan poise combines pity and indignation; in his ironic concern for the characters in his moral drama, his insistence on the precise pathology of their maladies *and* the sad uncertainty of our own health, he demonstrates both the clarity of his "general doctrine" of morality and the persistence of "direct fellow-feeling" that alone can keep the moralist's voice a human voice as well.

4

Satire and the Grotesque

THE *Imitations of Horace,* which date from the decade between 1730 and 1740, show remarkable things happening to Pope's poetic manner. In some ways the association of these satires with the example of Horace is misleading. A remark of John Dennis in *To Matthew Prior, Esq; Upon the Roman Satirists* (1721) pinpoints the difficulty:

> *Horace* argues, insinuates, engages, rallies, smiles; *Juvenal* exclaims, apostrophizes, exaggerates, lashes, stabbs. There is in *Horace* almost every where an agreeable Mixture of good Sense, and of true Pleasantry, so that he has every where the principle Qualities of an excellent Comick Poet. And there is almost every where in *Juvenal,* Anger, Indignation, Rage, Disdain, and the violent Emotions and vehement Style of Tragedy.[1]

By this definition, Pope's "Horatian" poems are often decidedly un-Horatian in manner. He found in Horace a wealth of satiric subjects and devices, but his "imitation" is essentially a remaking of his models along lines that are often as Juvenalian as they are Horatian.[2]

It is clear that Pope and his readers immensely enjoyed the resemblances between the social problems of Augustan Rome and those of Augustan England. If the faults were the same, the virtues might also correspond, and such a correspondence was the primary assumption of the neoclassic posture, the eighteenth-century man's cherished picture of himself in the *toga virilis.* To afford such pleasure, however, the literary imitation had to succeed imaginatively; the proof of the parallel is in the poetic life of the English version. We are, no doubt, finally more interested in the *Epistle to Arbuthnot* and the *Epilogue to the Satires* than in the satires that have direct sources in Horace. But even the latter have been remade, and they are best approached as poems in their own right. Though the structure of topics and events follows Horace closely, the details have usually been so transformed and pointed as to be Pope's own, as in this passage on the punishment of adulterers from *Sober Advice from Horace* (*Sat. I ii*):

> See good Sir *George* of ragged Livery stript,
> By worthier Footmen pist upon and whipt!
> Plunder'd by Thieves, or Lawyers which is worse,
> One bleeds in Person, and one bleeds in Purse;
> This meets a Blanket, and that meets a Cudgel—
> And all applaud the Justice—All, but *Budgel.*
>
> (55–60)

The first couplet stems from Horace's blunt *hunc perminxerunt calones,* but "Sir George" belongs as firmly to the contemporary English scene as does the cacophony of "Cudgel-Budgel." The significant detail of his being disguised as a footman to pursue his amours in secret is new: he pretends to change his status when he stoops to actions unworthy of it, but his pretense becomes his real condition; and he is punished by his inferiors, who could not have touched him had he kept to his proper role. The corrupt "high" suffers almost ritualistic befouling from the more virtuous "low," and the hierarchial disorder—Pope's main theme in the *Imitations*—is symbolically put right.

The *Imitations of Horace* show Pope engaged in a difficult task of poetic self-definition. Given a society that desperately needs satiric correction, who is the satirist to be? How should he talk? What personal attitudes and public stances are appropriate to his task? The first imitation, *Satire II i* (1733), addressed to William Fortesque, begins to suggest a solution in its use of the Horatian dialogue form. In the *Moral Essays,* despite Warburton's editing, the suggestions of dialogue play a minor part, because the conversations bring together views that essentially agree; but in the *Imitations* dialogue plays off attitudes that are in serious conflict. Although the opposing views usually reach some sort of equilibrium, the final agreement is ironic, and the growing distance between the dramatized "Pope" and his interlocutors indicates a significant change of method. In *Satire II i* Fortesque is the sympathetic but discreet adviser, counseling Pope to stop writing or at least switch over to the normal, safe mode of literary flattery that will pay off in "a *Knighthood,* or the *Bays*" (22). But Pope is helpless— "Fools rush into my Head, and so I write" (14). Like Shippen or Montaigne he cannot withhold his thoughts even to conceal his own flaws: "In me what Spots (for Spots I have) appear, / Will prove at least the Medium must be clear" (55–56). Satire is a lens between the poet and his world, and it reveals faithfully the defects on either side. As Pope himself once put it: "The best way to prove the clearness of our mind is by shewing its faults; as when a stream discovers the dirt at the bottom, it convinces us of the transparency and purity of the water." [3] The satirist's honesty about himself measures his compulsive devotion to truth: "In Durance, Exile, Bedlam, or the Mint, / Like *Lee* or *Budgell,* I will Rhyme and Print" (99–100). His morality is virtually a natural force, and so he may seem foolish or even mad to his prudent friends. He lacks a firm social status; like the Shakespearean clown, he can afford to blurt out things that more respectable people may find disconcertingly true.

His enemies include the same corruptors of nature encountered in *Bathurst*— "Thieves, Supercargoes, Sharpers, and Directors" (72). And Fortesque's strongest warning presents a dire picture of the financial world pooling its resources against this irritating foe: "Plums and Directors, *Shylock* and his Wife, / Will club their Testers, now, to take your Life!" (103–104). Despite the joke about avarice—"testers" are either very old coins or relatively valueless ones—the main point is still the abstractness of their lives; the "club" they may use on Pope is not a cudgel but a financial pool. Still, such thematic connections with the *Moral Essays* are combined with a new and radical view of the poet and his social role. He is "un-plac'd, un-pension'd, no Man's Heir, or Slave," and this independence allows him to "brand the bold Front of shameless, guilty Men" and "bare the mean Heart that lurks beneath a Star" (100–115) without troubling to be cautious or discreet. He does not pretend to the courage of Dryden or Boileau, who had a great deal to lose, but even a simple man like himself can criticize a social order he himself has so little part in. (The pose of humility of course expresses the most powerful sort of pride—who would *want* a part in such a world?) This is more than simple rejection of society. Pope's satire begins with the Augustan double vision, which combines belief that the ideals of his culture are true and good with a recognition that many of the forms of that culture have been drained of their ideal vitality. The satirist stands just outside the actual society, but he stands squarely within another order, composed of good men from every class, in which the ideal values are preserved and toward which the satiric rhetoric urges society itself to move.

The poet's ideal society is closely associated with rural nature:

Know, all the distant Din that World can keep
Rolls o'er my *Grotto*, and but sooths my Sleep.
There, my Retreat the best Companions
grace,
Chiefs, out of War, and Statesmen, out of
Place. (*Sat. II i,* 123–126)

This of course derives from the Horatian theme of withdrawal from the confusion and corruption of urban life to the peaceful sanity of the Sabine farm; but Pope's imitation draws authority from the withdrawal that was a real part of his own life. The villa at Twickenham was itself an imitation of Horace. What may have begun as mere obedience to the laws barring Catholics from permanent residence in London ended as a self-conscious but meaningful effort to live in the old Augustan manner. Friends like Bolingbroke and Peterborough *were* great men, and Pope's easy association with them proved that the official distinctions of birth and rank did not define the most important kinds of human relations. The truly great man remains great even when "out of place" like the satirist, and the man who has no "place"—the Catholic son of a linen merchant, who makes his living solely by writing—can, if his talents and personal qualities are sufficient, mingle with the great on equal terms. The ideal society is "natural" in two senses; its setting is country retirement, and its relationships ignore artificial distinctions. Pope asserts his place in an order that nullifies ordinary social categories with understandable pride:

Envy must own, I live among the Great,
No Pimp of Pleasure, and no Spy of State . . .
To help who want, to forward who excel;
This, all who know me, know; who love me,
tell;
And who unknown defame me, let them be
Scriblers or Peers, alike are *Mob* to me.
(133–140)

The conclusion of *Satire II i,* however, shows the difficulty of maintaining this position. Fortesque admits the persuasiveness of Pope's plea, but he reminds him that "Laws are explain'd by Men" and that his writings will be judged by their effect on the existing social order—there are statutes against Libels and Satires. Pope has a cunning answer:

> *Libels* and *Satires!* lawless Things indeed!
> But grave *Epistles,* bringing Vice to light,
> Such as a *King* might read, a *Bishop* write,
> Such as Sir *Robert* would approve—
> *F.* Indeed?
> The Case is alter'd—you may then proceed.
> In such a Cause the Plaintiff will be hiss'd,
> My Lords the Judges laugh, and you're dis-
> miss'd. (150–156)

This wry joke returns the poem to reality. For all Pope's fine talk about the private society to which alone he admits obligations, only the powers that *be* can save him from prosecution. The official scale still prevails in matters of public concern. The pastoral society of merit has not yet displaced the city-world of established social formalism; the law depends not on justice but on the attitude of George II or Walpole or whoever stands at the top of the ladder. The rural moralist remains a rustic clown in the eyes of the worldly, and the irony of the satirist's role cannot be resolved. Country nature in the *Imitations,* however, does more than locate the satirist's perspective of innocent shrewdness and associate it with an aristocracy of merit. Immediately after a passage in the "Murray" satire (*Epistle I vi,* 63–109) that shows wealth and innovation to be corruptors of virtue, we find this:

> Up, up! cries Gluttony, 'tis break of day,
> Go drive the Deer, and drag the finny-prey;
> With hounds and horns go hunt an Appetite—
> So Russel did, but could not eat at night,

Call'd happy Dog! the Beggar at his door,
And envy'd Thirst and Hunger to the Poor.
(112–117)

This is a "version of pastoral," but with an ironic twist to the Empsonian sense. Russel can't feel hunger and thirst, and he supposes the poor must be happy because they can. The simple life is best, after all. But Pope sees that thirst and hunger are good only when they can be satisfied—the poor are as miserable in their way as Russel is in his. "Happy Dog" both sentimentalizes the beggar and reveals the frivolous snobbery of Russel's vocabulary. Empson's formula—"from seeing the two sorts of people combined like this you thought better of both; the best parts of both were used" [4]—gets reversed: the *worst* parts of both define a social crisis. The toughness of Pope's irony can be measured by comparing Edward Young's treatment of the same problem: "High stations tumult, but not bliss, create: / None think the great unhappy, but the great" (*The Universal Passion,* I, 237–238). That is, they think they're unhappy, and they *are,* which is simpleminded and smug by Pope's standard.

The isolation from substantial experience, as in the *Moral Essays,* provides the *Imitations* with a moral norm. Pope's treatment of the theme ranges from the frivolous to the serious. The racy *Sober Advice from Horace* (*Sat. I ii*) explores the perversity of cultivated lust, which transforms sex from healthy pleasure into an imaginative disease whose only substantial result is pain or financial ruin for the lover who will "run to Perils, Sword, and Law, / All for a Thing [he] ne're so much as *saw*" (135–136). But while *Sober Advice* need not be taken very solemnly, the appeal to nature is elsewhere serious enough. There is the merchant whom "the spectre of pale Poverty" drives to "burn through the Tropic, freeze beneath the Pole" (*Ep. I i,* 69–72); and the misers:

. . . some farm the Poor-box, some the Pews;
Some keep Assemblies, and wou'd keep the
Stews . . .
While with the silent gowth of ten per Cent,
In Dirt and darkness hundreds stink content.

(*Ep. I i,* 128–133)

The "agricultural" language recalls the alternative to such squalor, the simple productive life on some Sabine farm. Nature harbored the perfect society before "Times corrupt" perverted social harmony and made satire necessary (*To Augustus,* 241–248), and it remains available as sustenance to simple, immediate wants:

From yon old wallnut-tree a show'r shall fall;
And grapes, long-lingring on my only wall,
And figs, from standard and Espalier join:
The dev'l is in you if you cannot dine.

(*Sat. II ii,* 145–148)

Give me, I cry'd (enough for me)
My Bread, and Independency!
So bought an Annual Rent or two,
And liv'd—just as you see I do. . . .
A little House, with Trees a-row,
And like its Master, very low.

(*Ep. I vii,* 69–78)

This last may seem to hedge a little—as he cannot very well till the soil himself, a gentleman needs a rent or two to live on. But this is just the point. Pope's rural nostalgia is not sentimental primitivism but a sophisticated impulse to recreate the original goodness of society. The scornful passage (*Sat. II ii,* 49–60) about the Wortley Montagus shows that meanness remains itself regardless of place; the country has no therapeutic power. It is simply the place where virtue can be sure of itself.

The natural life thus is chiefly a metaphor, a role that the poet would assume, compounded of the Horatian poet-in-retirement and the rural aristocrat of the native English tradition. Some posing in all this cannot be denied, but though the role is far from unflattering to Pope, it expresses more than personal vanity. The satirist can get no leverage from within the decadent society he attacks. He must achieve outside society an identity that embodies the values society lacks. The satiric identity of natural aristocrat is partly fact and partly a deliberate and necessay fiction; and Pope accepts and uses the lingering possibility that the natural man may be a clown as well as an aristocrat. He expresses a dream that is no less his own for having also been the dream of Horace. Parts of the dream are real, but another, less tractable reality opposes and mocks it at every turn; the alienation of the moral norm from the existing social "average" produces an increasing strain in the poet's voice.

The Satirist as Hero

The poet's conflict with his world gives unity to the *Imitations of Horace*. Seen from outside, society has crudely dissociated "distinction" from moral worth:

> There, London's voice: "Get Mony, Mony
> still!
> "And then let Virtue follow, if she will."
> This, this the saving doctrine, preach'd to all
> From low St. James's up to high St. Paul.
> (*Ep. I i*, 79–82)

An accurate moral language would keep clear the distinction between "salvation" and "savings." But one need not measure this society from outside to see the blurring of judgment that characterizes it. Even money is not a firm source of effective status, since "the Poor have the same itch" as the wealthy for constant changes of style and environment (*Ep. I i*, 152–160). Upper and lower become indistinguishably silly, or worse:

> But if to Pow'r and Place your Passion lye,
> If in the Pomp of Life consist the Joy;

Then hire a Slave, (or if you will, a Lord)
To do the Honours, and to give the Word . . .
"This may be troublesome, is near the Chair;
"That makes three Members, this can chuse a
May'r."
Instructed thus, you bow, embrace, protest,
Adopt him Son, or Cozen at the least,
Then turn about, and laugh at your own Jest.

(*Ep. I vi,* 97–109)

"Or if you will, a Lord" identifies the confusion: "if you prefer, hire a Lord instead of a slave"; or, "if you choose to *call* him that." In this crumbling order slaves are hard to tell from lords, and flunkeys (titled or otherwise) govern the conduct of their nominal betters. The solid familial relationships of a stable society dissolve when one invents parodies of them as a joke or a political stratagem. We foresee the dreadful Triumph of Vice in the *Epilogue to the Satires* (I, 157–158), where "thronging Millions to the Pagod run, / And offer Country, Parent, Wife, or Son."

As the "Fortesque" satire shows, Pope opposes to this corrupt reality his moral ideal of the private society of true merit. But the ideal seems tenuous when translated into practical possibility—the effective social reform that satire theoretically aims at—and increasingly we hear that the satirist is losing his Augustan poise. The drama of the magnificent *Epilogue to the Satires* (1738) in fact relies on the collision of blunt moral speech with a more equivocal, temporizing utterance that recalls Pope's earlier Augustan voice. *"Fr."* (the anonymous friend who serves as *adversarius* [5] in the two dialogues) complains about Pope's directness, and his own talk nicely demonstrates the "sly, polite, insinuating stile" of the "artful Manager" Horace which he recommends to the poet (I, 19–22):

To Vice and Folly to confine the jest,
Sets half the world, God knows, against the
rest;

Did not the Sneer of more impartial men
At Sense and Virtue, balance all agen. (I, 57–60)

The metaphor of balance, which in the *Essay on Man* and the *Moral Essays* expressed positive alternatives to the apparent chaos of immediate experience, now figures as an argument against the poet's position. *Fr.* is not imperceptive, but it is enough for him to relish in private the amusing discrepancies between "official" and real virtue. He seems a virtual caricature of the Dryden of *Religio Laici,* preferring common quiet to dangerous controversy over unreal issues. In him Pope gives his mature assessment of the cool, disengaged urbanity of an Addison or a Shaftesbury, which had been an ideal of his own earlier days: " 'Tis not enough your Counsel still be true, / Blunt Truths more Mischief than nice Falshoods do" (*Essay on Criticism,* 572–573). *Fr.* presents himself as a realist. His theme, like the (at least professed) theme of Mandeville, is the inevitable and useful imperfection of things as they are. His voice, at times indulgent and avuncular, at times maliciously feline, at times shrill with shock at Pope's plain speaking, is the familiar voice of intelligence debilitated by too much knowledge, sophistication that marks not moral subtlety but Gerontion-like moral paralysis.

This speaker is more than a convenient straw man. Both *Fr.* and *P.* are versions of Pope himself, or of any man aware of the conflict between his social identity and his secret image of himself as autonomous moral hero. The dialogue form articulates the inner debate between that part of us which "knows better" and that other part which will brook no compromises of its passionate commitment to truth. Pope controls both voices, of course, but the *Epilogue* moves not toward an Augustan reconciliation but toward acceptance of *P.*'s view, in all its extravagant exaggeration.

The two dialogues of the *Epilogue* develop various responses to the politic voice of *Fr.* Until late in the poem the mode of *Dialogue I* is ironic in the textbook sense: *P.* pretends to defend "the dignity of Vice," and the terms of the defense reveal the speciousness of justifying things as they are. If, as *Fr.* insists, the crimes of the wellborn are not to be dwelt upon by the satirist, the job still remains of keeping distinct the separation between classes. The vulgar are imitating the sins of their betters with intolerable cheek: Cibber's son "swear[s] like a Lord," Ward "draw[s] Contracts with a Statesman's skill," Bond and Peter Walter "pay their Debts [and] keep their Faith like Kings" (that is, not at all). The joke is clear enough. We condemn them, but not because we snobbishly think that they may become *better* than they should be. In this topsy-turvy society the highest are the worst; plebeians have quite as much inclination to vice, but they are normally saved by a lack of style; criminal know-how ought to be confined to the upper classes, where one expects it and is prepared to cope with it.

But the indirections of irony fail to undermine *Fr.*'s complacence, and toward the end of the dialogue *P.* is driven to a more open kind of speaking. Virtue is classless, he remarks, and need not concern him— "She's still the same, belov'd, contented thing" whether she "dwell in a Monk, or light upon a King." (We note the barbed difference between dwelling and lighting upon.) But Vice is "undone, if she forgets her Birth, / And stoops from Angels to the Dregs of Earth." The bitterness of "Angels" marks a change of tone; conversational give-and-take fades away in the concluding lines (145–172) of the first dialogue, the chilling vision of the Triumph of Vice. The everyday world is revealed as an Inferno; every human activity blurs into an ugly parody of itself as cultivated irony is abandoned and *P.*'s voice trembles with shock and rage. *Fr.*'s "political" view of a reality sustained and ordered by opposing evils has been a delusion. The oxymorons of Vice—innocence is shame and villainy sacred—are only blunter versions of the moral evasions and mystifications that *Fr.* has more elegantly advocated. In the final couplet the debate between *Fr.* and *P.*, the political man and the moral hero, has in fact been transcended: "Yet may this Verse (if such a Verse remain) / Show there was one who held it in disdain." The dramatic fiction of "dialogue" is deliberately broken—this has been a poem, "verse" and not life. Anger and disgust shatter artistic illusion, feeling takes precedence over mere form, and we see Pope finally not as poetic maker but as passionate human being. By asserting his independence of a corrupt social reality he defines his own isolation; his lonely voice rejects the world in order to maintain his moral integrity.

Pope's satiric protagonist is essentially an heroic figure, and he has to endure the ironies of his situation that Shakespeare explores so uncompromisingly in *Coriolanus*. Both Coriolanus and *P.* confront a disparity between the moral ego and the demands made upon it by political and social facts. Each experiences these demands impatiently, in the arrogant assurance that his personal "nature" affords a surer measure of truth and right than does the politic compromising of Menenius or *Fr.* And at the moment of crisis, each turns upon the political world and banishes *it,* in a gesture of superb integrity and equally of supreme absurdity. We are made to feel the virtue of single-mindedness even as we yearn for signs of ambivalence, for the discovery of the middle ground where education takes place in the recognition and pondering of both the reality and the incompatibility of conflicting motives. In the *Epilogue* Pope dramatizes himself as heroic clown, but in a more knowing way than does Coriolanus. Pope's satirist is both Coriolanus and Shakespeare, in effect, understanding the comic possibilities of moral heroism even as he insists on being a moral hero.

The conclusion of *Dialogue I* is equivalent to Coriolanus' insistence that "there is a world elsewhere"; *Dialogue II* recalls his awful discovery that there is no such thing. Again Pope begins in the mode of ironic indirection, as if to make one last try at preserving his balance. The satirist would be a hunter of vice, but in the face of the *adversarius*' knowledgeable explanation of the game laws the dignity of this role evaporates, and he is left as a kind of frustrated poacher, ruefully asking if there isn't *some* prey he may legally take. Again, however, such irony is inadequate to the gravity of the problem, and *P.*'s voice again takes on the inflections of the serio-comic moral hero who doggedly follows virtue whether she points "to Priest or Elder, Whig or Tory, / Or round a Quaker's Beaver cast a Glory" (96–97). The absurdity of the image is not to be minimized; by urbane, "cultivated" standards this involuntary morality is amusingly close to madness, and Pope knows it. But to express such intense conviction one can only shrug off laughter and keep on talking:

> Enough for half the Greatest of these days
> To 'scape my Censure, not expect my Praise:
> Are they not rich? what more can they pretend?
> Dare they to hope a Poet for their Friend?
> (112–115)

This is more than personal egotism. The "I" of the poem is not simply the man but the man as poet, with the poet's claim to dignity and virtue that are qualities of his craft and not just of his personality. But there is anxiety in the pride. Compared with the immediacy of heroic action, poetry is a pretty unsubstantial weapon and vice a Protean object, and Pope's arrogance seems partly defensive, an exorcising of Vice by a willful affirmation of faith in Virtue:

> Ask you what Provocation I have had?
> The strong Antipathy of Good to Bad.
> When Truth or Virtue an Affront endures,
> Th' Affront is mine, my Friend, and should be yours.
> Mine, as a Foe profess'd to false Pretence,
> Who think a Coxcomb's Honour like his Sense;

Mine, as a Friend to ev'ry worthy mind;
And mine as Man, who feel for all mankind.

(197–204)

P. stubbornly resists complication and moral subtlety. There is Good and there is Bad—the capitalizing of abstract nouns never did stronger service—and their antipathy has the natural inevitability of magnetism. But antipathy is a defensive feeling, and *P.*'s image of himself as some almost Promethean sufferer for "all mankind" shows how far he has been driven from the confident, ironic modesty that is the Horatian satirist's normal air:

Fr. You're strangely proud.
P. So proud, I am no Slave:
So impudent, I own myself no Knave:
So odd, my Country's Ruin makes me grave.
Yes, I am proud; I must be proud to see
Men not afraid of God, afraid of me:
Safe from the Bar, the Pulpit, and the Throne,
Yet touch'd and sham'd by *Ridicule* alone.

(205–211)

Like Coriolanus he seems "a thing / Made by some other deity than Nature, / That shapes man better"; yet for all its loftiness this is an oddly minimal statement. Even the slightest distaste for servility is pride by the standards of this world, and the tone is rueful in its arrogance.

Still, the positive aspects of this pride are impressive. If he has been driven into this ultimate position, the ground he now occupies is the center of his case, which no longer needs to be qualified and compromised. The satirist, no longer able to speak simply as a man among men, projects himself as God's deputy, trying not by persuasion but by sheer intensity of will to make an impious society right the imbalance between its values and divine ones. His "sacred Weapon" finds its "Heav'n-directed" target in the blasphemy of official distinctions, "all that makes Saints of Queens, and Gods of Kings."

And his heroic intensity nullifies the earlier Triumph of Vice with a vision of Virtue:

> . . . diadem'd with Rays divine,
> Touch'd with the Flame that breaks from Virtue's Shrine,
> Her Priestless Muse forbids the Good to dye,
> And opes the Temple of Eternity. (232–235)

The permanence of art, treated with some unsureness in *The Temple of Fame,* now gets eloquent assertion. Immortality rewards artistic virtue, and while it is figurative immortality rather than literal, the petty achievements of the worldly cannot earn it. The true moral scale transcends time and death, and the poet speaks for a power that is ideal and eternal:

> Let Envy howl while Heav'n's whole Chorus sings,
> And bark at Honour not confer'd by Kings;
> Let Flatt'ry sickening see the Incense rise,
> Sweet to the World, and grateful to the Skies:
> Truth guards the Poet, sanctifies the line,
> And makes Immortal, Verse as mean as mine.
> (242–247)

But Pope recognizes, quite as clearly as Shakespeare, the ironies that adhere to the heroic identification of self with natural virtue. The grand assurance of tone cannot disguise the fact that this assertion of the artist's unique moral dignity is a virtual confession of defeat. Heroism is a function of alienation. Like any hero, Coriolanus grows more awesome and mysterious as his loyalties to other people or extrapersonal causes drop away; he is most himself (most unlike *us*) at the moment of his death, when he has finally detached himself from every external limit to his freedom. (His death is in effect a metaphor for the moral suicide his attempts to *preserve* his moral identity have caused.) Pope's satirist would not need to glorify his role so insistently if every other kind of virtue had not disappeared from his world.

He simply has no one to talk to. The select, understanding interlocutors to whom the *Moral Essays* and the *Imitations of Horace* were largely addressed have been replaced by the anonymous and hopelessly cynical "Friend," who in the ways that count is no friend at all. The dialogue has become an oration, in fact a harangue, addressed to anyone who will listen, and this provides a final twist of bitter comedy:

> Yes, the last Pen for Freedom let me draw,
> When Truth stands trembling on the edge of Law:
> Here, Last of *Britons!* let your Names be read;
> Are none, none living? let me praise the Dead,
> And for that Cause which made your Fathers shine,
> Fall, by the Votes of their degen'rate Line!
> *Fr.* Alas! alas! pray end what you began,
> And write next winter more *Essays on Man.*
>
> (248–255)

The grand tone has grown almost too grand. ("Pen" and "Votes" in this context are perilously close to bathos.) And the discovery that the good men are all dead—that the celebration of virtue must be an elegy—produces a faltering of the voice that is close to the double-take of farce. Yet even this approach to absurdity cannot stop the last furious assertion of integrity.

Truth and Law, the two vocabularies with which the *Imitations of Horace* have dealt, come into open conflict, and it may be Truth that is the weaker. "Pope is thinking once more of the threatened censorship of the press," Mr. Butt says,[6] but that particular legal hazard reflects a broader and more shocking suppression of personal virtue by an entrenched and corrupt public order. There is honest feeling in Pope's final note to the poem:

> This was the last poem of the kind printed by our author, with a resolution to publish no more; but to enter thus, in the most plain and solemn manner

> he could, a sort of PROTEST against that insuperable corruption and depravity of manners, which he had been so unhappy as to live to see. Could he have hoped to have amended any, he had continued those attacks; but bad men were grown so shameless and so powerful, that Ridicule was become as unsafe as it was ineffectual.

Both the defiance and the frustration of this note are clear in the poem's last lines. Like the Friend, we recognize that *P.* has gone too far; such extravagance is probably as futile as it is uncivilized. But unlike *Fr.*, we know that what has happened in these dialogues is worth any number of cautiously generalized essays in moral definition. It is true that Pope's presentation of *P.* recognizes and explores the *comic* aspects of the Coriolanus-like moral hero, the man who will not compromise his vision of experience even though the world leaves him no positive alternative to bitterness. Yet we surely respond to *P.* with a warm approval that Shakespeare forbids us to feel about Coriolanus. Although we recognize that heroism may be as absurd as it is venerable, and as dangerous, the recognition tellingly defines the price of perfect virtue. The price is painfully high; to pay it one may have to abandon the ironic defenses of urbane civility and expose oneself to ridicule. But though it is one thing to be a fool because you *are* one, in all innocence, it is quite another to decide that seeming a fool is preferable to the moral evasions into which urbanity can lead. Readers of Blake and the "mad" poems of Yeats should have no trouble in recognizing Pope's satiric identity, or in understanding that, for all its eccentricity and exaggeration, it expresses a moral intelligence that is complex and final.

The Grotesque Mode

The new poetic mode of the Horatian satires is in part determined by generic considerations; satire traditionally allows a less decorous and impersonal speech than do the "higher" genres. But Pope's decision to stoop to truth and moralize his song must have been impelled by a genuine need to represent experience in a different, more violent way. Suprisingly often he turns his comparatively urbane Horatian models into "paraphrases" that are, in detail and over-all effect, anything but urbane:

> Slander or Poyson, dread from *Delia*'s Rage,
> Hard Words or Hanging, if your Judge be *Page;*
> From furious *Sappho* scarce a milder Fate,
> P—x'd by her Love, or libell'd by her Hate:
> Its proper Pow'r to hurt, each Creature feels,
> Bulls aim their horns, and Asses lift their heels,
> 'Tis a Bear's Talent not to kick, but hug,
> And no man wonders he's not stung by Pug:
> So drink with *Waters,* or with *Chartres* eat,
> They'll never poison you, they'll only cheat.
>
> (*Sat. II i,* 81–90)

Except for the couplet on Sappho, the cues for everything in this passage are in the Horatian source, yet Pope's version seems intense, harsh in tone, compared with the cool, explanatory amusement of the original. It is partly the difference between Horace's relatively relaxed hexameters and pope's tensely antithetical couplets, but Pope spent the last fifteen years of his life perfecting the couplet's resources for expressing just this kind of feeling.

The animal imagery is adapted from Horace, but it points to a kind of language that dominates the *Epistle to Arbuthnot* and the *Epilogue,* where Pope has a free hand. Animals in the *Pastorals* and *Windsor Forest* were idealized exemplifications of natural innocence, as they are in the *Essay on Man* and *Bathurst,* where they indicate the dignity of nature as against the depravity of bad men. But in the *Imitations* Pope picks up the view advanced in the first *Dunciad,* that bad men are not different from animals but like them: Avidien and his wife are dog and bitch (*Sat. II ii,* 49); both "Lord Fanny" (*Sat. II i,* 6) and the Grub Street hack (*Ep. to Arbuth.,* 89) are spiders; profligates return from their orgies "transform'd to Beasts" (*Ep. I vi,* 122); bishops and peers are steers and packhorses (*1740,* 69); Sporus is butterfly, wasp, spaniel, toad, and snake all in one (*Ep. to Arbuth.,* 308–333). Such comparisons are of course traditional in satire; the images point scornfully at deviations from the best human possibilities, and the irony remains positively "operative," in the Jamesian sense—it "implies and projects the possible other case, the case rich and edifying where the actuality is pretentious and vain." [7] To this extent we are still in the realm of Augustan technique.

But the gusto with which Pope frequently explores the distasteful details of such comparisons suggest that a view of nature as moral chaos is impinging upon the view of it as moral norm, as in this passage from the *Epilogue* (II), in which Pope defends his taunting of Lord Hervey about the dubious authorship of his Latin epitaph on Queen Caroline:

> *P.* Faith it imports not much from whom it came,
> Whoever borrow'd, could not be to blame,
> Since the whole House did afterwards the same:
> Let Courtly Wits to Wits afford supply,
> As Hog to Hog in Huts of *Westphaly;*
> If one, thro' Nature's Bounty or his Lord's,
> Has what the frugal, dirty soil affords,
> From him the next receives it, thick or thin,
> As pure a Mess almost as it came in;
> The blessed Benefit, not there confin'd,
> Drops to the third who nuzzles close behind;
> From tail to mouth, they feed, and they carouse;
> The last, full fairly gives it to the *House.*

Fr. This filthy Simile, this beastly Line,
Quite turns my Stomach—*P.* So does Flatt'ry mine;
And all your Courtly Civet-Cats can vent,
Perfume to you, to me is Excrement. (168–184)

P.'s offhand indifference vanishes in the fierce obscenity, and by Augustan standards of social and poetic decorum the *adversarius*' objection seems fair. The analogy would cut more insolently if it were merely suggested, and Pope's delight in the details of the figure magnifies the petty occasion out of all reasonable proportion; it is a filthy simile, and *P.*'s final rejoinder seems petulant and lame. Yet the passage is alive in a way that Augustan verse can hardly be. There comes a time when urbanity cannot cope with evil, and it may be dangerous to discriminate between minor evil and major. The satirist can express his shock at such deviation from the norm only by himself departing from it in the other direction. Cultivated discourse cannot do full justice to vileness—like the stable boys who befouled "good Sir George," Pope's obscenity objectifies the spiritual filth behind the disguises of evil.

The art of such a passage is above all "dramatic"; we follow the voice of a "Pope" who is a creation of literary resources and not simply the poet himself. But it seems clear that the materials from which the dramatized "Pope" is made are more than fictive. "Incongruity" is the key to these satires; I have shown some of the ways Pope pairs unlike things within the large opposition of nature and society; and his characteristic rhetorical device, the antithesis, is obviously a perfect instrument for expressing the incongruous. The incongruity of *The Rape of the Lock* is essentially comic: social frivolity is projected against pastoral and heroic backgrounds to make it ridiculous. We can laugh at Belinda without ceasing to love her because she is *smaller* than she might be. "Humor," as Kenneth Burke says, "specializes in incongruities; but by its trick of 'conversion downwards,' by its stylistic ways for assuring us in dwarfing the magnitude of obstacles or threats, it provides us relief in laughter." As we move through the *Moral Essays* and the *Imitations of Horace,* however, our laughter becomes more and more uneasy as Pope's tone grows increasingly sardonic and his imagery less and less decorous. As a convenient name for such a change, Mr. Burke proposes "grotesque," which he defines as "incongruity without the laughter":

> The grotesque comes to the fore when confusion in the forensic pattern gives more prominence to the subjective elements of imagery than to the objective, or public, elements. One could probably analyze any art, even the most classically clear, and find there such motives as the pit, symbolic castration, rebirth, the *mystic* awe of light. But when the public frame erected above these primitive responses is broken, the essence stands more clearly revealed. The symbolic quality is revealed more clearly, precisely because the forensic superstructure erected above it is less firm.[8]

To apply this definition to Pope of course requires some adjusting. Although there is something like the "mystic awe of light" in the *Dunciad,* it is not necessary in Pope's case to pursue very far Mr. Burke's connection of the grotesque with mysticism, and such Ur-motives as castration and rebirth may be left to the consideration of some future psychiatric interpreter. Yet the general idea of the "grotesque" may help to explain certain qualities of Pope's later poetic manner. In the passage about the Hogs of Westphaly, for example, his subjective interest in his imagery does seem to overcome his sense of the public decorum his audience was accustomed to find even in so impure a genre as satire. His increasing willingness to disturb the dramatic propriety of his poems suggests that such propriety, as conventionally defined, could not adequately contain the feelings he wanted to incorporate. And it is tempting to speculate that this kind of disturbance indicates a growing doubt in the ability of "public" intellectual structures —all the content and overtones of such words as "decorum," "society," "reason," and "order"—to control the tendency of men and nature to become disorganized and mad. (By an amusing etymological accident, the Italian *grottesco* is derived from the word for "grotto," that symbol of Pope's personal withdrawal from the public world.)

Certainly the Horatian poems are grotesque in some common senses of the term. They show Pope increasingly willing to deal with certain unpleasant physical realities that would have represented dangerous breaches of decorum in most of his earlier poems:

> And Peers give way, exalted as they are,
> Ev'n to their own S-r-v—nce in a Carr.
>
> (*Ep. II ii,* 106–107)

> *Oldfield,* with more than Harpy throat en-
> du'd,
> Cries, "Send me, Gods! a whole Hog *bar-
> becu'd!*"
> Oh blast it, South-winds! till a stench exhale,
> Rank as the ripeness of a Rabbit's tail.
>
> (*Sat. II ii,* 25–28)

> While with the silent growth of ten per Cent,
> In Dirt and darkness hundreds stink content.
>
> (*Ep. I i,* 132–133)

> The stomach (cram'd from ev'ry dish,
> A Tomb of boil'd, and roast, and flesh, and
> fish,
> Where Bile, and wind, and phlegm, and acid
> jar,
> And all the Man is one intestine war).
>
> (*Sat. II ii,* 69–72)

Rufa's at either end a Common-Shoar,
Sweet *Moll* and *Jack* are Civet-Cat and
Boar. . . .
While bashful *Jenny*, ev'n at Morning-Prayer,
Spreads her Fore-Buttocks to the Navel bare.
(*Sober Advice*, 29–34)

The first of these passages is wholly Pope's invention, and the others stem from comparatively discreet suggestions in Horace. It is not a matter simply of referring to such details, but of pointing to them with such descriptive gusto. To be sure, the contrast with the decorum of Pope's earlier poems is in part deceptive, since they observe the more restricted proprieties of genres other than satire; Pope may not outdo some of the English satirists (Donne and Marston, for example) in grotesquerie, but he does seem to strain even the loose standards of decorum of Horatian satire, the tradition that he was most consciously following and to which his readers were attuned.

A less obvious kind of grotesquerie seems to be emerging in the treatment of death as it affects man and nature:

Let rising Granaries and Temples here,
There mingled Farms and Pyramids appear,
Link Towns to Towns with Avenues of Oak,
Enclose whole Downs in Walls, 'tis all a joke!
Inexorable Death shall level all,
And Trees, and Stones, and Farms, and
Farmer fall. (*Ep. II ii*, 258–263)

"This subtle Thief of Life, this paltry Time" (*Ep. II ii*, 76) is seen as the inescapable enemy of man and his whole existence in nature, and the classical confidence in natural morality, which eased the terror of such knowledge in the *Moral Essays*, has weakened. The bitterness of " 'tis all a joke" and the almost surrealistic grimness of the last line are not in Horace—Pope's own feelings are wholly engaged in this "imitation."

"Grotesque" thus names any indication, in image, tone, or theme, that the poetic speaker finds the Augustan tension between the ideal and the actual hard to sustain. Another way of putting it is to say that Pope exercises his *public* role as poet less confidently. He must increasingly remind us, through direct reference to his own life or through eccentric quirks of speech, that he is a "real person" as well as a poet, and that the demands of personality are often more powerful than professional decorum. In *The Rape of the Lock* and the *Epistle to Burlington,* the great masterpieces of his Augustan manner, the conventional medium is wholly adequate to express the range of feeling the poet brings to it. He can say all he has to say within the limits of his chosen manner. In the later poems, however, the trend is away from this union of convention and feeling, and toward an art in which personal experience, violent and idiosyncratic, tends to be too powerful for the "forensic superstructure" of the poem's avowed form to bear. This trend is clearest in the satires that have no direct source in Horace. In the *Epilogue* the satirist's feelings constantly threaten to break out of the poem, as his voice falls into ironic despair and rises to furious honesty in an almost helpless rhythm. In *Dialogue II,* especially, these shifts of tone make up the real poetic structure. But the *Epistle to Arbuthnot* may best reveal the full significance of Pope's grotesque satiric mode.

Persona and Personality

The *Epistle to Arbuthnot* is a pastiche, incorporating fragments written at various times for various occasions, such as the portrait of Atticus and the lines on Pope's mother. Though as a consequence it lacks the most obvious kinds of formal order,[9] Pope is able to give it unity by his careful management of tone. We are as much interested in Pope, or the speaker who bears his name, as we are in the people he talks about; and the epistle achieves its form in our fascinated observation of his struggle to retain his individuality and dignity in a chaotic world of fools, knaves, and madmen: "Fire in each eye, and Papers in each hand, / They rave, recite, and madden round the land" (5–6). This amused mock desperation will not persist for long; madness and hurly-burly are the "normal" conditions of this world, and the poet's patience gets sorely tried before the poem is over.

The epistle's recurrent animal imagery, of the most degrading sort, expresses a grotesque distortion of social and esthetic order. Wakefield noted a parallel between Pope's comment on textual scholarship—

> Pretty! in Amber to observe the forms
> Of hairs, or straws, or dirt, or grubs, or worms;
> The things, we know, are neither rich nor rare,
> But wonder how the Devil they got there?
> (169–172)

—and William Walsh's *Elegy to his Mistress:*

> Verse can give fame, can fading beauties save,
> And, after death, redeem them from the grave:
> Enbalm'd in verse, thro' distant times they come,
> Preserv'd, like bees, within an *amber* tomb.[10]

To the reader who recalled Walsh's lines (or any of the numerous equally conventional treatments of the idea), Pope's use of the "preservation in amber" image would seem especially pointed. Walsh's bees have no meaning apart from their setting, but Pope's grubs and worms remain nasty despite their surprising position. In fact, their inappropriateness to the amber makes them even more unpleasant than usual, just as Bentley's and Theobald's emendations of Milton and Shakespeare seem even stupider in contrast to the works which they deface. Pope's passage is grotesque in a double sense: it plays on the incongruity between a beautiful substance and disgusting insects, and it deliberately distorts the "poetic" feeling one expects to be evoked by a natural mystery.

The physical and moral grotesquerie of the world Pope describes in *Arbuthnot* justifies the role he plays in the poem. His persona is the "plain good man driven to write satire,"[11] but the effectiveness of the mask depends upon our sense of what he is driven *by*—a deformity of values that pervades the whole literary world, from rhyming Peers like Sporus on down to Ambrose Philips, who "turns a *Persian* Tale for half a crown" (the normal wage for prostitution) and the poor compulsive scribbler "who lock'd from Ink and Paper, scrawls / With desp'rate Charcoal round his darken'd walls." And the epistle deals with more than literary folly. The sin of the scribblers is not just that they write badly: they are bad (stupid, sick, dishonest, insane) men. Pope attacks Grub Street and the Court on more than personal grounds; the literary war stands for the whole death struggle between natural moral intelligence and the unnatural mindlessness that seeks to reduce intelligence to the chaos of stupidity. But the violence of the poem casts some doubt on the assumption that moral intelligence *is* natural—could nature be on the side of the scribblers?

Such an uncertainty seems to underlie the epistle's over-all rhythm of emotion, in which passages asserting and praising the satirist's own dignity and control alternate with passages where this cultivated discipline of self gives way to violent expressions of anger and outrage. The passage beginning "Friend to my life" (27) shows this rhythm nicely. Pope starts with conversation, modestly minimizing his own achievements ("many an idle Song") and ruefully complaining of a disease Arbuthnot may not be able to cure:

> What *Drop* or *Nostrum* can this Plague remove?

Or which must end me, a Fool's Wrath or
Love?
A dire Dilemma! either way I'm sped,
If Foes, they write, if Friends, they read me
dead.

The touch is light, and the dire dilemma is too neatly defined syntactically to be entirely credible; the aloof, mock-analytical manner only asserts his superiority. Yet he can't speak falsely, for all his cool good will—he "can't be silent, and [he] will not lye." This tension between well-mannered benevolence, on the one hand, and dogged devotion to principle on the other, leads to some agony: he sits "with sad Civility," with "honest anguish, and an aking head." Yet the discomfort scarcely seems very urgent. It is another way of showing his superiority to his thick-skinned tormentors. Nothing disturbs this equanimity until Arbuthnot warns him that his simile about asses' ears may be dangerous (75–78), whereupon some of his composure deserts him:

" 'Tis nothing"—Nothing? if they bite and
kick?
Out with it, *Dunciad!* let the secret pass,
That secret to each Fool, that he's an Ass.

This new tone of genuine irritation and contempt continues through the passages on Codrus and the spider-scribblers, before it gradually subsides after line 95 into the old mode of controlled scorn. It is significant that after the initial address to Arbuthnot the discourse moves from social speech into a kind of simple narrative, and only when the disturbance begins in the "Midas' ears" section does the speaker return to his dramatic situation: "And is not mine, my Friend, a sorer case, / When ev'ry Coxcomb perks them in my face?" He begins to feel a real grievance, and he couches it as an appeal for personal sympathy, an appeal that, when the sympathy is not forthcoming, yields to anger.

This rising and falling of emotion, from equanimity to

violence and back again, characterizes the movement of the whole poem. The passages on Pope's childhood and literary debut (125–156) show a serene consciousness of being in the right, with infrequent disturbances being confined to the individual couplet and resolved within it:

> Yet then did *Gildon* draw his venal quill;
> I wish'd the man a dinner, and sate still:
> Yet then did *Dennis* rave in furious fret;
> I never answer'd, I was not in debt.

The rhetorical syntax of the parallel "Yet then" clauses is soothed by the simple declarative order of the responses. But the thought of the critics who have attacked him brings an outburst of emotion, climaxing in the scathing denunciation of "Each Wight who reads not, and but scans and spells, / Each Word-catcher that lives on syllables," and the worms-in-amber passage, before it relapses into the old urbanity: "Were others angry? I excus'd them too; / Well might they rage; I gave them but their due" (173–174). There follows the portrait of Atticus, the finest example in the poem of Pope's use of the controlled, man-of-good-will role, but its judicious coolness soon gives way to a bitter attack on "Wits and Witlings" ("Nor like a Puppy daggled thro' the Town, / To fetch and carry Sing-song up and down"), which in turn yields to controlled contempt in the portrait of Bufo.

After a return to complete restraint and dignity in the lament for Gay and the modest self-congratulation of "I was not born for Courts or great Affairs," the voice slowly rises (283–304) through contempt ("That Fop whose pride affects a Patron's name") and indignation ("And sees at *Cannons* what was never there") to the introduction of Sporus:

> A Lash like mine no honest man shall dread,
> But all such babling blockheads in his stead.
> Let *Sporus* tremble . . . (303–305)

The lofty assertion of the satirist's respect for genuine

virtue breaks up in the angry alliteration of "babling blockheads" and the ominous rise of the voice at the start of the new couplet.

The portrait of Sporus is the peak in this series of emotive curves that gives the poem its structure. It begins within the framework of dialogue:

> Let *Sporus* tremble— "What? that Thing of silk,
> "*Sporus,* that mere white Curd of Ass's milk?
> "Satire or Sense alas! can *Sporus* feel?
> Who breaks a Butterfly upon a Wheel?"
> Yet let me flap this Bug . . .

Arbuthnot tries to forestall the explosion—his cool contempt indicates an imperturbably Augustan confidence in standards of judgment and a gentlemanly sureness of superiority to those who do not measure up. But the "Pope" of this poem, like the *P.* of the *Epilogue,* will not be restrained. Sporus is immune to satire or sense, but Pope, gripped by the strong antipathy of good to bad, must flap him anyway. No real good can come of it, but the inner pressure of moral horror defies containment.

Virtually all the qualities of the grotesque mode figure in this astonishing passage of vituperative invention. Sporus is a "bug" who "stinks and stings," a "well-bred Spaniel," a "familiar Toad" who "spits himself abroad," an "Amphibious Thing" who, though he shows a "Cherub's face," is "a Reptile all the rest." These images of physical and moral distortion, with their formulation in paradox and oxymoron, sum up the "vile Antithesis" that is Sporus, whose elusive essence cannot be fixed by the public, judicial operations of logic. Pope's anger explodes into metaphor, as in the daring identification of Sporus-Hervey with the original of all evil—"at the ear of *Eve,* familiar Toad." "Familiar" focuses the ironic richness of Pope's disgust: Sporus is intolerably cheeky in his hobnobbing with royalty; he is a toady not only by profession but by family; like a "familiar spirit" he comes to serve but may stay to corrupt; he is seen there with tiresome regularity; he is that well-known toad who whispered into the ear of the sleeping Eve. This disgust permeates even the sound of the verse; Mr. Mack notes the "concentration of sibilants and labials" in a general spitting sound,[12] and one notes too the frequency of hard monosyllabic words: flap, bug, dirt, stinks, stings, buzz, spits, spite, smut, etc. The abrupt, ejaculatory rhythms that result create a tone far removed from the easy fluency of Augustan style. The fertility of poetic invention proves the intensity of the feelings that are being dramatized.

The structure of emotive curves encourages belief in the reality of the dramatic personality that addresses Arbuthnot and ourselves; the inability of the urbanely superior speaking manner to suppress strong emotion adds to the sense that a human being is talking. The deliberate shattering of one persona—the self-contained, confidently contemptuous man of the world—makes possible the creation of another, more important identity, that of a recognizably human speaker, to whom vice is unbearably repugnant and whose response to wickedness is reassuringly violent and intense. Such humanity of reaction makes a striking contrast to the scribblers and patrons, who are incapable of honest emotion. Atticus lives his life on one colorless level—he is a "tim'rous foe, and a suspicious friend," which is to say that his feelings are so uniform as not to be feelings at all. Sporus is empty; his reactions are wholly formed by his surroundings as he squeaks, like a proper courtier, in obedience to the ventriloquist Expediency; he could never be guilty of the honest indiscretion of his enemy. The scribblers themselves are mechanical men—the Drury Lane bard "rhymes ere he wakes," and his clock-like fellows find their "secret standard" in "that Casting-weight Pride adds to Emptiness." Being half-dead already, they are happily insensitive to any external stimulus:

Let Peals of Laughter, *Codrus!* round thee
break,
Thou unconcern'd canst hear the mighty
Crack.
Pit, Box, and Gall'ry in convulsions hurl'd,
Thou standst unshook amidst a bursting
World. (85–88)

Pope has in mind Addison's translation of Horace's *Ode III iii* (7–8), and the heroic endurance there described does find a perverse kind of likeness in Codrus' amiable stupidity, his indifference to any standards but his own. But the situation is wrong; the vast epic arena has become opening-night at Drury Lane, the "convulsions" the hero-author faces are convulsions of jeering laughter, and Codrus' defiance of the audience demonstrates only his conceited insensitivity. Like the spider, who "spins the slight, self-pleasing thread anew" whenever his web is broken (89–92), the scribbler is guided in his "dirty work" not by feeling but by mindless, subhuman instinct. The contrast between such automatons and Pope's poetic speaker, who can discriminate intelligently *and* rise to overwhelming moral emotions, needs no comment.

The *Epistle to Dr. Arbuthnot,* then, achieves unity through Pope's ability to invent and control a voice that moves convincingly through all the ranges of tone between cool urbanity and violent moral indignation. This voice has its comic aspects—like Blake, Pope knows the potency of the old image of the truth-teller as fool—but the end effect is not comedy but grotesquerie. The satirist can lose his temper, and though this marks his superiority both to impervious coxcombs like Sporus and bland "administrators" like *Fr.,* we know that he can never see in himself the gratifying mastery of reality that they see in themselves all the time. And despite the now common idea that Pope creates in his verse a persona, a mask of rhetoric that is not the "real" personality of the writer,[13] the "Pope" of these poems is much more than a fiction by which the real Pope manipulates his materials and his readers. Manipulation (by any name) suggests evasiveness or—as often in Swift—uncertainty about where one really is. As a critical metaphor, for all its value in discrediting naïvely "biographical" interpretation, the mask emphasizes concealment and subterfuge rather more than it suggests the creation of imaginative roles for the artist himself. At its noble best rhetoric is an agent of responsibility, a means of clarifying the issues at stake. To move us, the poet or the orator should be moved himself, and his rhetoric should *reveal* his feelings as hesitant, tangled ordinary speech so seldom can. The "mask" in Pope's satires is not a false face but an identity quite as real as any of the poet's other identities; it is fashioned not so that critics may admire its workmanship but so that readers may better understand the motives that made the poems necessary. The "Pope" of *Arbuthnot,* the *Epilogue,* and the other Horatian satires *is* Pope—Pope provisionally freed from the irksome restraints of social and political moderation so that his deepest commitments may get something like pure expression. The *adversarii* are Pope too, but in them are combined and punished just those elements of civilized Augustan personality that necessarily yet tragically thwart that best self we can never quite become. Pope the man could never quite live up to the passionate morality of his satiric self—his biography is full of the troubles he got into by trying—but the persona of the *Imitations* remains as a moving imaginative version of the troubled human presence within it.

By straining the framework of social and poetic propriety Pope left behind him a great art, the Augustan balance achieved so splendidly in *Windsor Forest, The Rape of the Lock,* and the *Epistle to Burlington.* But by doing so he created another kind of art, less pure and structurally less "perfect," which stands in relation to the Augustan poems much as *The Winter's Tale* stands to, say, *Twelfth Night.* The great Augustan myth of the union of ideal and actual is increasingly strained in the late poems; James's "rich and edifying" other case never disappears entirely from the verse, but the gap between it and the "pretentious and vain" actuality becomes steadily wider. (There is little obvious grotesquerie in *To Augustus,* for example; but when the poem is read in the context of the other *Imitations of Horace,* its ironic surface urbanity may be seen as an earned alternative to a more violent kind of expression, and the dignity and seriousness of Pope's criticisms of contemporary politics and letters can better be appreciated.) Pope avoids the breakdown that Dr. Leavis has diagnosed in the irony of Swift, "the spectacle of creative powers . . . exhibited consistently in negation and rejection," [14] but the dramatic emphasis in the later verse centers around the enormous personal effort that must be made to bridge the gap between things as they are and the (hopefully) possible other case revealed by moral vision. Pope's poetic solution for the problem is what I have called the grotesque mode, but its very nature emphasizes the terrible slimness of the hope.

5

The Uncreating Word

THE END and the climax of Pope's poetic career is the *Dunciad* of 1743. The complex history of the poem is outlined in the Twickenham edition and interpreted in Aubrey L. Williams' useful study; [1] I shall largely ignore this history, in an attempt to see how the *Dunciad* that most people read fits into the account I am making of Pope's poetic development. My view is that the earlier versions in three books, though showing many of the features of theme and manner that I discuss, do not wholly put them to use. The poem needs the Fourth Book, and especially the fuller dimension it gives to the famous conclusion, which in the 1729 version seems oddly out of place at the end of Book III. Apart from its obvious use as a personal weapon, the three-book version seems to me largely an experiment in developing the mock epic's resources for grotesquerie; its poetic details express little more than local satiric meanings, but in the 1743 version these details fall into place in a larger and far more serious imaginative pattern.

The World Turned Upside Down

Although the simple joke at the heart of the *Dunciad* is the same joke Pope used in *The Rape of the Lock*—the language you ordinarily use to describe the largest and best people you can conceive of is disastrously inappropriate for describing small, bad people—still in the

Dunciad the effect of the joke has obviously changed. A characteristic passage startlingly reverses the normal process of purity yielding to decay:

> Thro' Lud's fam'd gates, along the well-known Fleet
> Rolls the black troop, and overshades the street,
> 'Till show'rs of Sermons, Characters, Essays,
> In circling fleeces whiten all the ways:
> So clouds replenish'd from some bog below,
> Mount in dark volumes, and descend in snow.
> (II, 359–364)

The simile invites a complex response, combining revulsion from the Dunces' swampy corruption, wonder at their stupid but stubborn perseverance (it must be hard to make even fake snow from such dirty material), pleasure in the poetic power that can bring a kind of beauty out of such ugliness, and amusement that the comparison is used at all. This last feeling, however, differs from the amusement evoked by epic parody in *The Rape of the Lock;* while the *Dunciad* has a beauty of its own, it is far from the beauty of small, glittering things found in Belinda's world. Laughter at clouds being replenished from bogs will be just a little nervous —this incongruity is not "comic" but "grotesque."

Such uncomfortable juxtapositions of the pleasant and the ugly run through the poem. The remarkably profuse animal imagery elaborately relates the world of the Dunces to the lower orders of creation; and although in part we feel superior because we are human, reasonable, and so forth, we must at the same time concede the Dunces a certain brainless but disturbingly potent vitality. Pope in other ways suggests that they have lost any meaningful relation to ordinary human nature. The world of Dulness is full of monstrous distortion. In Book I (81–84) the goddess proudly reviews her "wild creation" of "momentary monsters," who are elsewhere compared to statues and machines. If they retain a semblance of humanity, some flaw will mark them as Dulness' own, as in the case of the "meagre, muse-rid mope, adust and thin" (II, 37), Defoe earless in the pillory (II, 147), or the Virtuoso who is "canker'd as his Coins" (IV, 349); if, despite all their efforts, they still look human, they are much embarrassed (IV, 525–528). The richest vein of distortion runs in the allusions to monstrous births and perverse familial relationships, for Dulness is the "Mighty Mother," and her maternity implies a ghastly subversion of the normal processes of conception and growth: "Here she beholds the Chaos dark and deep, / Where nameless Somethings in their causes sleep" (I, 55–56). The reference is to *literary* deformity, but the imagery invites a response that seems too strong for the reference. We are to shrink from bad writing as urgently as from unnatural birth and growth.

The most famous (and most often deplored) kind of ugliness in the *Dunciad* is the obscenity, the way in which Pope dwells upon the excretory processes and debased sexuality. The delicate sexual innuendoes of *The Rape of the Lock* give way to vigorous expressions of interest in the obscene and all its details:

> Renew'd by ordure's sympathetic force,
> As oil'd with magic juices for the course,
> Vig'rous he rises; from th' effluvia strong
> Imbides new life, and scours and stinks along;
> Re-passes Lintot, vindicates the race,
> Nor heeds the brown dishonours of his face.
>
> (II, 103–108)

The elegant irony of "sympathetic," the mouth-filling Latinate diction, and the neat epic parody in "brown dishonours" [2] combine in a deceptive sonority of movement that makes the bite of "scours and stinks" and "brown" especially impolite. Pope's artistry struggles with our revulsion and subdues it, and the result is richly poetic; but though we may laugh at Curll to avoid some more painful response, the idea of a human being drawing sustenance from filth is scarcely "comic." The struggle between tonal dignity and conceptual ugliness produces a grotesque imaginative violence that would have torn *The Rape of the Lock* to pieces. As in the *Imitations of Horace,* personal feeling interferes with decorous public speech.

Despite such interference, of course, the *Dunciad* is more than a study in ugliness. The poem is poised between alternatives. On the one hand, the deformed, depraved world of Grub Street may stand as an image of the actual world we ourselves inhabit, or of what it will become if dullness prevails. At the same time, however, Pope leaves open the possibility that Grub Street may be a special case, a limited world surrounded by pleasanter realms of order. It is the verse, especially, that provides this positive assertion:

> So (fam'd like thee for turbulence and
> horns)
> Eridanus his humble fountain scorns;
> Thro' half the heav'ns he pours th' exalted
> urn;
> His rapid waters in their passage burn.
>
> (II, 181–184)

The beautiful elevation and movement of the last line modulates the indecency of the action and the further obscene suggestion in "burn" (which "Scriblerus" carefully underlines in a note). It is as though Pope could not help but write beautifully, whatever the occasion. As Dr. Leavis says, the beauty of such a passage

> is inseparable from the whole habit of versification. . . . When Pope is preoccupied with the metrical structure, the weight, and the pattern of his couplets, he is bringing to bear on his "materials" habits of thought and feeling, and habits of ordering thought and feeling. The habits are those of a great and ardent representative of Augustan civilization.[3]

One might add that these "habits" serve a pertinent dramatic purpose. The ability to find beauty in ugliness, without obscuring the fact that it *is* ugly, demonstrates the highest sort of intelligent civilization, and it triumphantly asserts Pope's superiority to his victims. Dunces make ugliness from beauty, and the difference between their activity and the contrary activity embodied in the verse itself marks the distinction between anarchy and order.

The positive undercurrent finds expression in a number of ways. Pope plays off Grub Street ugliness against the heroic dignity of classical epic, the artfully beautiful innocence of pastoral, the rich fertility of actual nature, and the moral seriousness of the classical and Christian intellectual traditions. Such contrasts both underline the squalor of the Dunces' habits and enhance the gravity of their offense, which is in effect an attempt to subvert cultural and natural order.

The Orders of Light

The contrast between the ugliness of Dulness and the beauty of moral intelligence may be taken as the main theme of the *Dunciad.* It figures, as I have suggested, as a stylistic principle operating in individual passages —for example, when an obscene image is balanced by a "classical" tone or rhythm. But the contrast, in one form or another, plays a larger part than this in the poem. One of its embodiments, in the recurrent imagery of light and darkness, may suggest that the final four-book version of the *Dunciad* has a kind of wholeness that so many readers have denied to it.[4]

The key to this pattern is of course the famous conclusion, in which Pope suddenly abandons the elaborate fictions of mock epic and the detachment of the impersonal narrator. At line 627 of Book IV the Dunces vanish as the poet shifts his attention from the puny creatures of Dulness to the larger philosophical implications of intellectual and moral disorder. The dominant tone has been vituperative mockery; but every reader senses in the conclusion a deepening and darkening of mood, a retreat from irony in the face of the ultimate destruction of reason and humanistic value. The reader no longer enjoys the security of merely observing; Pope adopts direct address and the present tense to emphasize our involvement in what nonsense finally means. He loses a certain dramatic neatness by transferring this prophetic speech from Settle, who spoke it at the end of the three-book versions, to the anonymous narrator of the poem, but there is a heightening of seriousness that is well worth the sacrifice. When Settle says it you tend not to believe him—it all seems a slopping over of a Dunce's deranged imagination; but when it is spoken by the narrator himself, and so backed by all the resources of feeling that have generated the poem, it cannot be so easily dismissed.

Although the word itself is mentioned only once, "light" is obviously the metaphor upon which the conclusion (627–656) is based. The advancing power of Dulness puts out the lights of art and science. First "fancy," to the Augustans a lower faculty but (as even Hobbes admitted) an essential one, is blotted out: "Before her, *Fancy*'s gilded clouds decay, / And all its varying Rain-bows die away." [5] "Wit" too "shoots in vain its momentary fires" before "the meteor drops, and in a flash expires." [6] In each case Pope emphasizes both the ephemeral quality of the phenomena and their naturalness; clouds and meteors can't really be expected to last, and yet somehow they *should*. One by one all the arts by which man illuminates his existence are extinguished, and the end is utter blackness. "Light dies before thy uncreating word"—the light of Genesis and the *Logos* of St. John are obliterated by this new and blasphemous un-Creation. Dulness destroys all order, until, in the brilliant theatrical analogy with which the poem ends, the curtain falls on the universal drama, and both audience and players are buried in darkness. "Drama," the transformation of otherwise random occurences into "history" or "theology" or any other understood pattern of physical or spiritual relations, is the ultimate achievement of human culture, and this final darkness quite literally buries "*All.*"

The emphasis on darkness in this conclusion can be related to the rest of the poem through an interesting couplet. When Dulness reigns supreme, "Nor *public* Flame, nor *private,* dares to shine; / Nor *human* Spark is left, nor Glimpse *divine!*" (IV, 651–652). The italics are Pope's, and as these are the only adjectives so emphasized in the poem, we should take them seriously. A hierarchy of terms is suggested. The light of "private" intellectual activity, the fleeting illumination cast by the powers of the individual mind, did not stand particularly high in the Augustan scale of values, as a glance at *Religio Laici* (1–22) or Swift's annihilation of *both* reason and imagination in *A Tale of a Tub* (Section IX) will show. The extinguishing of "public" flame is more serious; the Augustan concern for maintaining an intelligible community of ideas and beliefs is well known, and the arts, which link the present with the traditions of the past, were of vital importance in fixing private perceptions in a public form. But Dulness goes even further. The encroaching darkness that obliterates every "human Spark," public and private, also obscures the "Glimpse divine," the imperfect but enriching vision of a higher light of which any human spark is only a reflection.[7] Light, in short, has various significances, but in whatever form it appears it expresses something about the fundamental structure of values in reality.

Dulness herself, the chief figure in the 1743 version, is characteristically enveloped in mists or clouds, and Cibber's prayer to her— "And lest we err by Wit's wild dancing light, / Secure us kindly in our native night" (I, 175–176)—shows why: wit and light are the same, and so the true Dunce prefers his *native* night and the uterine security it affords. Intelligence is painful, and from his point of view the best alternative to the dancing, dazzling illumination of wit is not steady light but total darkness. Dulness represents the power of passive mindlessness, the emblems of which are darkness and sleep.

Her aura of mist and vapor in part magnifies the goddess; "A veil of fogs dilates her awful face" (I, 262)—she is majestic and terrifying because one can't see her true size and shape clearly.[8] But her obscurity also ridicules her, for she herself cannot see through the veil, which isolates her from reality and understanding. A series of "massing" and "blotting out" images show how she and her children seek to extend the blessings of darkness to others:

> Thro' Lud's fam'd gates, along the well-known Fleet
> Rolls the black troop, and overshades the street. (II, 359–360)

> As thick as bees o'er vernal blossoms fly,
> As thick as eggs at Ward in Pillory.
> (III, 33–34)

> Prompt at the call, around the Goddess roll
> Broad hats, and hoods, and caps, a sable shoal:
> Thick and more thick the black blockade extends. (IV, 189–191)

> Then thick as Locusts black'ning all the ground. (IV, 397)

Each passage (and there are others) makes its satiric comment on the developing action, but each also contributes to a larger meaning: Dunces obscure light, even without trying, and their most trivial actions may demonstrate this symbolic characteristic.

The light imagery relates the "ugliness" of the *Dunciad* to its positive content. Much of the obscenity, for instance, associates the Dunces' love of filth with a love of darkness and concealment, as in the cloacal revelry of the diving contest in Book II. If light is an enemy, then darkness and dirt are friends, and all sorts of filth will seem congenial to a Dunce. The frequent references to animals commonly associated with darkness, dirt, submersion, or burrowing work to a similar effect. The vituperation takes on a certain rhetorical dignity from such imagery: it is easy enough to call your enemies animals or filth-lovers, but when the aspersions fit into a larger, almost philosophical pattern, the sense of personal malice lessens.

Though the Dunces themselves cast light of a sort, their illumination differs significantly from the radiances of intelligible order:

> His Peers shine round him with reflected
> grace,
> New edge their dulness, and new bronze their
> face.
> So from the Sun's broad beam, in shallow urns
> Heav'ns twinkling Sparks draw light, and
> point their horns. (II, 9–12)

The clue is "shine." Their light is harsh and glaring; and they gleam not with their own brilliance but with reflected light that illuminates nothing. Like mirrors, they remain cold even while they seem bright and warm by stealing light from other sources—and they deceive themselves as well as others:

> Kind Self-conceit to some her glass applies,
> Which no one looks in with another's eyes;
> But as the Flatt'rer or Dependant paint,
> Beholds himself a Patriot, Chief, or Saint.
> On others Int'rest her gay liv'ry flings,
> Int'rest, that waves on Party-colour'd wings:
> Turn'd to the Sun, she casts a thousand dyes,
> And, as she turns, the colours fall or rise.
> (IV, 533–540)

Pope here recalls Belinda's sylphs with exquisite effect, but behind the effect stands the sharp criticism carried by the whole light and dark pattern.

False seeing is in fact one of Dulness' most powerful weapons, as she demonstrates in the "heroic" games. She forms a poet out of air for whom her publisher-children compete, but when the victorious Curll tries to claim his prize, "it melted from his sight, / Like forms in clouds, or visions of the night" (II, 111–112). The effect is comic, but the prediction of the poem's conclusion, where "*Fancy*'s gilded clouds decay," carries ominous overtones. Dulness' power to make something of nothing foreshadows her final making nothing of everything. It is only a short imaginative step to the "re-creation" of the universe into garish parodies of its proper form:

> She, tinsel'd o'er in robes of varying hues,
> With self-applause her wild creation views;
> Sees momentary monsters rise and fall,
> And with her own fools-colours gilds them all.
>
> (I, 81–84)

The cosmic grotesquerie of Cibber's vision (III, 231–272) and the final extinction of order fulfill this pattern, as Dulness becomes a blaspheming disrupter of the divinely wrought structure of reality. Out of local jokes emerges the completion of the "private-public-divine" hierarchy.

Light, which I have treated as "imagery," comes in the *Dunciad* to carry the consistency and intensity of meaning ordinarily called "symbolic." Pope evokes responses to the dualism of light and darkness that are instinctive—"archetypal"—and not just socially and satirically useful. Light is the means by which we locate ourselves and direct our actions, in contrast to darkness, in which we know neither what we are doing nor where we are. Pope's imagery brings various common metaphors to mind—"see the light," "bright as day," and so forth—and the feeling involved in such comparisons of mystery to understanding enlarges the poem's scope. It is no coincidence that the Augustans generally seem to have agreed that sight, though in some ways the most abstract of the senses and the least understood, was nevertheless the most immediate in its psychological effect and the most costly to lose—an agreement in which we probably concur.[9]

Such general symbolic values stand behind the light imagery in the *Dunciad,* and the feelings they evoke support Pope's special attitudes throughout. There are all kinds of light, and the "private-public-divine" hierarchy provides a paradigm of the poem's whole rhetorical structure. It can be read as a personal attack on the poet's enemies, as a defense of an ethical ideal against wholesale stupidity, or as a warning that a threat exists to the divine architecture of the universe. Human order, Pope argues, with a famous tradition behind him, is an image of a more exalted order, and an attack on one menaces the other. We proceed up the ladder analogically. Behind the topical, satiric exterior lies symbol, and behind symbol the great myth of the uncreating word—the cosmic over-meaning, almost incredible out of context, expressed so powerfully by the conclusion. But the myth is not "asserted"—it develops implicitly from satiric details that have the charms of insolent immediacy. The full richness of Pope's technique will escape a reader who cannot respond simultaneously to comedy and seriousness.

One Dead Level

The organizing image of light thus expresses Pope's Augustan grasp of a positive moral order that stands behind and criticizes the "darkness" of human folly. Light is of course only one of a number of metaphors for this order that appear in the *Dunciad* (rising and falling, waking and sleeping, organic growth and decay are other important ones), but they all reveal a natural moral ideal that sustains the poet in an actuality almost wholly deformed. The ideal is, to be sure, more private than in a poem like the *Essay on Criticism,* and the appeal in the *Dunciad* to fantasy and grotesque symbolism foreshadows Blake's visionary poetic. But Pope retains his sense of a public, a class (however small) of readers who share his vision of order. What this means can be appreciated by thinking of *The Vanity of Human Wishes,* the greatest English neoclassic poem after Pope, where Johnson's apparent expectation of an audience that would question his point of view leads him to a rhetoric that for all its dignity and power seems at times uncomfortably hortatory. The creation of beauty and coherence out of ugly confusion is one of the great Augustan achievements, and the *Dunciad* is the last great English poem to have such a *shared* vision of order as its main expressive principle.

Yet there is an attitude in the poem that works against this Augustan quality. De Quincey nearly put his finger on the problem when he said that the last lines confused him:

> Do [present times] and their pursuits lead to [the victory of anarchy] as a possibility, or as a contingency upon certain habits which we have it in our power to erase (in which case this vision of dulness has a *practical* warning), or is it a mere necessity, one amongst the many changes attached to the cycle of human destiny, or which chance brings round with the revolutions of its wheel? All this Pope could not determine.[10]

Is the vision a prophecy, or a warning of state that *could* come about if the world failed to grow more reasonable? There can be no simple answer, but Pope's final position shows a certain pessimism pulling against the positive meanings.

Pope seems to have had two ideas about the relation of anarchy to order, two opposing myths about man's role in nature. The first, supporting the positive attitudes expressed in his poems, is essentially the classical concept of a Golden Age: that in the beginning the state of nature was perfect and peaceful, an Edenic time when man lived in harmony with nature and his fellow creatures in Arcadian tranquillity. This pastoral myth, upon which depend the "official" meanings of *Windsor Forest*, the *Essay on Man*, and the *Epistle to Burlington*, dramatizes the human desire to believe that experience is ultimately orderly, that the nature of reality is hierarchical design, and that sin is corrigible. It makes satire possible, for it justifies the belief that folly and wickedness are unnatural and that norms exist toward which moral education can work. In terms of our key image, it asserts that natural reality is "light," and that darkness represents a dangerous aberration from natural perfection. The opposing view was in Pope's day usually blamed on Hobbes: psychologically if not historically, the state of nature is a state of disorder and conflict; human beings attain the light of dignity and reason only with difficulty, and they are in constant danger of lapsing into darkness. (Hobbes, interestingly, was said to have been afraid of the dark.) [11] No direct influence need be postulated—about all we know of Pope's opinions about Hobbes is that he thought him a good reasoner and a bad translator of Homer; [12] but it seems clear that the hypothesis of man's essential goodness and nature's inherent congruence to human ideas did not fully satisfy Pope. A convenient modern name (which he would doubtless have hooted at) for this second view is "entropy," for it implies that nature, even when strenuously opposed by creative human intelligence, steadily tends to seek lower and lower levels of organization. We find in the *Dunciad* suggestions that nature is not entirely hostile to Dulness, that light may *not* be the ultimate reality, that the public structure of values Pope appeals to with such seeming confidence is in danger of collapsing.

We find, for one thing, that Dulness' "ancient right" dates from "eldest time," and that she is the daughter of "eternal Night" (I, 9–12); the germ of this idea can be found in the last of the lines Pope added to Wycherley's *Panegyrick on Dulness* in 1707: "So Wit, which most to scorn it does pretend, / With Dulness first began, in Dulness last must end." Much is made of the long tradition that stands behind the Dunces (I, 95 ff.); and while Pope is poking fun at them by comparing them with the bad writers of the past, they nevertheless assume a disturbing dignity from being part of a long historical series. In Cibber's vision (Book III), the portion of the globe under the influence of reason is said to be pitifully small, and the language expresses more feeling than we would expect from Settle, the fictitious narrator. The claims of Dulness to universal domination are not easy to refute.

The pervasive physical movement in the *Dunciad* is downwards. There are numerous references to diving and sinking of various sorts, as when Cibber, in the throes of composition,

> gnaw'd his pen, then dash'd it on the ground,
> Sinking from thought to thought, a vast profound!
> Plung'd for his sense, but found no bottom there. (I, 117–119)

His nonsense resembles "running Lead" that slips down through the cracks in his head (I, 123–124), and his wits, like lead bullets, manage to fly briefly but soon fall to earth (I, 181). The great diving contest forms the climax of the heroic games (II, 269–346), recalling Cibber's earlier pondering of a nobly selfless gesture: "Shall I, like Curtius, desp'rate in my zeal, / O'er head and ears plunge for the Commonweal?" (I, 209–210). Even the smallest kind of detail shows Pope's delight in this idea:

> As to soft gales top-heavy pines bow low
> Their heads, and lift them as they cease to blow:
> Thus oft they rear, and oft the head decline.
> (II, 391–393)

> Happier thy fortunes! like a rolling stone,
> Thy giddy dulness still shall lumber on.
> (III, 293–294)

> The gath'ring number, as it moves along,
> Involves a vast involuntary throng,
> Who gently drawn, and struggling less and less,
> Roll in her Vortex, and her pow'r confess.
> (IV, 81–84)

Dulness works like a natural force, exerting an all-engulfing gravitational pull that cannot be resisted. Everything declines into inertia, a curve completed by the falling curtain and universal burial of the final couplet. Mr. Empson says that "the idea behind *MacFlecknoe* and the *Dunciad* [is] that there is an ominous mystery in the way the lowest and most absurd things make an exact parallel with the highest." [13] This ominous quality is enhanced by the tendency of high things to slide downward and become their low counterparts, despite all the efforts of moral intelligence to keep them separated into their proper levels. Hierarchy collapses into sameness, light yields to darkness, as entropy continues.

In satiric terms, the downward movement attacks the "sinking" Pope had ridiculed in the *Peri Bathous,* but in the *Dunciad* he has more on his mind than bad writers' love for the bathetic. The sinking of the Dunces leads to repose and sleep, a kind of peace that Pope does not simply despise:

> Know, Eusden thirsts no more for sack or praise;
> He sleeps among the dull of ancient days;
> Safe, where no Critics damn, no duns molest,
> Where wretched Withers, Ward, and Gildon rest. (I, 293–296)

> No noise, no stir, no motion can'st thou make,
> Th' unconscious stream sleeps o'er thee like a lake. (II, 303–304)

> But in her Temple's last recess inclos'd,
> On Dulness' lap th' Anointed head repos'd.
> Him close she curtains round with Vapours blue,
> And soft besprinkles with Cimmerian dew.
>
> (III, 1–4)

The satiric edge never withdraws, but there is also a tenderness in the tone and even a kind of yearning. Darkness may bring a *welcome* end to the complexities of day; sleep and intelligence are in a sense antitheses, and yet the latter may often long for the former. As Pope remarked early in his career (again in the additions to Wycherley's *Panegyrick on Dulness*), dullness is "the safe Opiate of the Mind, / The last kind Refuge weary Wit can find."

The Dunces are thus to be envied, in a way. Untroubled by the cares and responsibilities of the reasonable man, they can yield happily to the tendency of life to run downhill toward darkness, sameness, and sleep. Pope puts into Bentley's mouth a couplet that succinctly describes the pedagogical aim of Dulness: "With the same Cement, ever sure to bind, / We bring to one dead level ev'ry mind" (IV, 267–268); and he later makes Thomas Gordon, a Whig journalist, redefine the process: "Now to thy gentle shadow all are shrunk, / All melted down, in Pension, or in Punk" (IV, 509–510). The aim of Dulness is sameness, the utter absence of the differentiation that makes order possible, as though the maternal Anarch were a ghastly literalization of the metaphor ascribed to Spinoza— "The purpose of Nature is to make men uniform, as children of a common mother." [14] In such a state intelligence has no place, for there are no qualitative differences to be discriminated. Dulness melts down and levels off the structural order of "degree" that had been the imagination's dream since the beginnings of thought.

Even the poet himself, the contemptuously detached speaker who records the saga of Dulness, cannot feel wholly secure. Among the chimeras with which the goddess fills Cibber's head at the beginning of Book III, along with "the Statesman's Scheme, / The air-built Castle, and the golden Dream," we find the "Poet's vision of eternal Fame." The irony may include Pope himself, it seems, and this supposition is confirmed at the start of Book IV:

Yet, yet a moment, one dim Ray of Light
Indulge, dread Chaos, and eternal Night!
  Of darkness visible so much be lent,
As half to shew, half veil the deep Intent.
Ye Pow'rs! whose Mysteries restor'd I sing,
To whom Time bears me on his rapid wing,
Suspend a while your Force inertly strong,
Then take at once the Poet and the Song.

"This astonishing poetry," which "triumphantly . . . enlists Milton into an Augustan sublime," [15] daringly introduces the poet into his mock poem, demanding a response that a casual reading of the *Dunciad* might not have anticipated. The speaker's comfortable superiority to his subject vanishes for a moment as he recognizes his own subjection to time's destructive power. Such recognition lends serious overtones to the theme of *literary* entropy, "Prose swell'd to verse, verse loit'ring into prose" (I, 274):

How Prologues into Prefaces decay,
And these to Notes are fritter'd quite away.
(I, 277–278)

"Leave not a foot of verse, a foot of stone,
A Page, a Grave, that they can call their own."
(IV, 127–128)

"Turn what they will to Verse, their toil is vain,
Critics like me shall make it Prose again."
(IV, 213–214)

The ring of sadness is more than a satiric device. The decay of literature mirrors the decay of nature: verse loiters into prose just as order lapses into chaos, light into darkness. Fame turns out to be doubly elusive, as the attitude that in *The Temple of Fame* remained a submerged possibility now comes to the surface of Pope's verse. Not only does the poet die, but he finds little likelihood that his work will long survive him. The poet's craft, that noble metaphor for human creativity in general, bows to the uncreating word of Dulness—both the poet and the song must yield to darkness and death.

A powerful vision of dissolution dominates the Fourth Book. As Pope's Argument says, "The Progress and Effects [of Dulness' final yawn] on all Orders of Men, and the Consummation of all, in the *Restoration* of Night and Chaos, conclude the Poem." The poem sings of Dulness' "Mysteries *restor'd*" (IV, 5), the return to the "Saturnian days of Lead and Gold" rather than to the genuinely Golden Age of pastoral myth. The goddess finally stands revealed as the deity of "Night *Primæval,* and of Chaos *old*" (IV, 630)—"Lo! thy dread Empire, CHAOS! is *restor'd*" (IV, 653). The origin of created order, to which it must return, is the eternal darkness of chaos; the idea is Miltonic,[16] but there is genuine feeling in Pope's use of it. The critical intelligence that made the poem possible must bow before the onslaught of *nature*—a nature no longer seen as a synonym for light and order but as a ceaseless mutability destroying everything that makes life dignified or even possible.

This "tragic" dimension of the *Dunciad* depends upon the resonances that the more consistently serious imaginative design of the Fourth Book strikes in what had been written earlier. The "sublimity" noted by Dr. Leavis is most evident in the invocation to Book IV and the conclusion, and it is such passages as these, when Pope draws most openly upon Miltonic resources, that bring the underlying seriousness of the other books to life. The poem in three books is narratively more tidy than the final version, just as the original *Rape of the Lock* is neater and more "exquisite" than the great poem Pope made from it; but it is the Fourth Book, with its open appeal to deep feeling and something like the "degree of horror" by which Edmund Burke was to identify the sublime, that withholds the poem from the limbo that received its many eighteenth-century imitations and preserves it as literature.

It would be easy, and wrong, to overstate the case. The "tragic" sublimity of the *Dunciad* is a tendency in the poem but not quite an accomplished fact. Its positive, Augustan meaning is not wholly overcome; the threatened decay of order, the triumph of entropy, remains a threat and not a certainty. Though it is severely strained, the tension between the ideal and the recognition that man's dark estate poses some awful challenges to ideals does not snap, for even the expressions of sublime terror and disgust remain within the bounds of Pope's Augustan style. He can make beauty out of fright, just as he can out of ugliness; the "habits of thought and feeling" embodied in his verse are strong enough to control and direct his vision of disorder. I should put it that in the *Dunciad* Pope's Augustanism meets its sharpest challenge from the actual world and conquers it; but the struggle, like Shakespeare's in the last plays, exhausted the medium of expression, and Augustan sensibility was never to triumph so finely again. There are great moments in the later Augustans, but for anything like the sustained achievement of the *Dunciad,* we must wait for Blake and his radical redefinition of the poetic act.

Conclusion

POPE'S CAREER, interpreted from the point of view this reading has adopted, falls into a kind of pattern. The Augustan style is in the early poems a way of expressing what Basil Willey has called "Cosmic Toryism,"[1] the belief that "nature" can best be conceived of as universal, regular, and ultimately moral, and that man can himself be moral if he knows its laws and models his behavior upon them. Although individual experiences of nature, and especially of its central principle of change (which for man is death), may suggest that it is indifferent to the human lot, the imagination can resist this idea by appealing to various myths of permanence. In Pope, any positive statement about experience implies that an opposing negative possibility has been faced and disciplined. He understood that no social or intellectual system fully describes reality, which always includes potentialities for tragedy. But he knew too that a reality conceived of as *wholly* tragic makes art impossible and life unendurable; the response to such a reality can only be silence, and art is the activity of breaking silences. Pope's Augustan mode is thus in essence a dialogue between "comic" myths of recurrence and "tragic" ideas of time's finality.

As Pope's career proceeds, the mythic opposition to silence becomes increasingly difficult to sustain. The biographer and literary psychiatrist might be of help here. To what extent was Pope's anxious reliance upon friendship and personal loyalty a condition of his physical suffering and his alienation from "normal" living? How strongly did he feel the political injustices (as he saw them) done to such friends as Atterbury and Bolingbroke? [2] How close is the relation of the deaths of his mother, Gay, and Arbuthnot, and the growing despair of Swift, to the darker mood that prevails in the later poems? But such questions are for those competent to answer them. Whatever the causes, the later poems show an increasing strain being exerted on the Augustan expressive manner by views of experience that are essentially "grotesque."

If this interpretation of Pope is at all valid, then some adjustments of the usual view of eighteenth-century literary history suggest themselves.[3] It is customary to see Pope as the greatest Augustan poet, the perfector of a poetic mode that—though it lingers on and finds some moments of glory in Johnson, and some moments of at least real distinction in Churchill, Goldsmith, Cowper, and Crabbe—is essentially completed as a literary instrument by the time Pope is through with it. The view of Pope as the normative Augustan seems to me true as far as it goes, but it does tend to draw a historical line between him and the great poets of the next age. (Even the notion of "ages" is a danger here.) And this line may obscure important affinities quite as much as it defines genuine differences.

Writers on Blake, for example—even such perceptive ones as Northrop Frye and Mark Schorer—have found in Pope a convenient figure to represent, for special purposes, the whole climate of literary practices and intellectual attitudes against which Blake rebelled.[4] The trouble is that the "Pope" of the Blakeans seems largely to consist of the earlier poems and especially the *Essay on Man*. I have tried to show that the *Essay*, read literally, is a dangerous source for determining

Pope's views of nature and man. If instead you compare Blake with the Pope of the *Epistle to Bathurst*, the *Epilogue to the Satires*, and the *Dunciad*, you get rather a different picture. You see, I think, that both men express profound discontent with the official attitudes of their societies, especially in "economic" matters. You see Pope, though certainly to a less radical extent, resorting to a personal abruptness of tone and a privacy of symbolism that suggests Blake far more than it does the other Augustans. You see that Pope's moralizing of his song led him eventually into grotesque fantasias, a process different only in degree from the way Blake's conventional early lyricism proceeded through the *Songs of Experience* to the grotesque fantasias of the Prophetic Books.

The similarities between Pope and Blake can of course be overemphasized quite as easily as they have usually been underemphasized. There is nothing in Pope equivalent to Blake's determined assault upon the foundations of a whole epistemology, and even in the areas where they are comparable it is usually a matter of seeing a tendency in Pope where you see a full realization in Blake. Pope remains an Augustan even as he questions the assumptions upon which his Augustanism depends. This is in fact his strength. Blake is a great lyric poet and a greater intellectual revolutionist, but in his most ambitious works, the Prophetic Books, the attempt to recreate epic is flawed by too narrowly Biblical a tone and by the hyperprivacy of the symbolic machinery. Even if one suspects some doctrinal animus in D. G. James's account of Blake's mythological muddles, it remains difficult to deny that Mr. James is often right.[5] Blake's theogony is confusing, though in his own mind it may not have been confused; his attempt at so radical a redefinition of values drove him into a privacy of vision—and more important, of expression—that denied him an audience. It is impossible to believe that

Blake was mad in any but a Philistine sense of the word, but it is hard to blame his contemporaries for supposing that he was.

Though he was driven toward a similar kind of privacy, Pope retained an audience. It was an increasingly small one, certainly; but as Milton observed, the audience fit for great poetry is apt to be few. Even at his most grotesque moments, when he dramatizes his poetic "self" at its highest pitch of eccentricity, alienation, or despair, Pope speaks to, for, and about a culture that was the imaginative and (in part) the substantial possession of real people, ones who knew that they possessed it and were grateful for it. Blake's contemporaries may have been *too* grateful, too uncritical of their tradition; when a culture is accepted mechanically it ceases to be valuable, but Pope (I have tried to show) knew this quite as well as Blake, and had in many respects more effective ways of saying so.

Austin Warren has said that Pope "felt the precariousness of civilization"; [6] he knew that civilization is not only an idea but an activity, the activity of putting properly together words and things that if left to themselves would rather remain separate. This activity is a form of love, and like all forms of love it is both difficult and necessary. "We love the things we love for what they are"—in his own terms Pope reiterates this rueful wisdom of Robert Frost, adding the proviso that if our love is to mean anything we must guarantee its force by also hating the things we hate for what *they* are. (It is an embarrassing message for a world of committees, councils, and associations, which prefers co-operating to discriminating.) Pope's poems state the identity of things without evasion, and so they are full of love, the love that cherishes its objects *because* they are imperfect and mortal. Like another great attempter of poetic systems for holding the world in a single imaginative whole, he came in time to apparent defeat:

Now that my ladder's gone,
I must lie down where all the ladders start,
In the foul rag-and-bone shop of the heart.[7]

But the defeat is only apparent. Like Yeats, Pope comes finally to accept his own vulnerability; he acknowledges, as Swift could never quite do, the unbreakable ties between noble principles and the essential if often unlovely and ignoble imperfections that unite us with other men. In his mediations between "myth" and "fact," his expression of both the necessity and the enormous difficulty of civilized love, he reminds us of who we are and what we're worth.

Notes

("*TE*" = Twickenham Edition: *The Poems of Alexander Pope*, ed. John Butt *et al.* [London, Methuen; New Haven, Yale University Press, 1939–1961] 6 vols.).

Preface

[1] W. B. Yeats, *Letters*, ed. Allan Wade (London, Rupert Hart-Davis, 1954), p. 310.

[2] Raymond Williams, *The Long Revolution* (London, Chatto and Windus, 1961), p. 260.

Chapter 1.

[1] For a statement of this view, see Joseph Wood Krutch, "Pope and Our Contemporaries," in *Pope and His Contemporaries: Essays Presented to George Sherburn*, ed. J. L. Clifford and L. A. Landa (Oxford, Clarendon Press, 1949), pp. 251–259.

[2] "If he had smiled why would he have smiled?

"To reflect that each one who enters imagines himself to be the first to enter whereas he is always the last term of a preceding series even if the first term of a succeeding one, each one imagining himself to be first, last, only and alone, whereas he is neither the first nor last nor only nor alone in a series originating in and repeated to infinity." James Joyce, *Ulysses* (New York, The Modern Library, 1934), p. 716.

[3] For an exhaustive study of *Windsor Forest* as a political poem based on the theme of *concordia discors*, see Earl R. Wasserman, *The Subtler Language* (Baltimore, Johns Hopkins Press, 1959), pp. 101–168. My reading had been worked out before Mr. Wasserman's appeared, but I have been encouraged by some general agreements between our views.

[4] For this pun, see Maynard Mack, "On Reading Pope," *College English*, VII (1946), 264–265.

[5] Bonamy Dobrée, "The Theme of Patriotism in the Poetry of the Early Eighteenth Century," *Proceedings of the British Academy,* XXXV (1949), 62–63.

[6] I owe this point, and much of my understanding of *Windsor Forest* as a whole, to David R. Ferry.

[7] For this passage and the tradition behind it, see Reuben A. Brower, *Alexander Pope: The Poetry of Allusion* (Oxford, Clarendon Press, 1959), pp. 45–48, 54–55, 57–58.

[8] For Mr. Wilson Knight's interpretation of *The Temple of Fame,* see his *Laureate of Peace* (London, Routledge and Kegan Paul, 1954), pp. 79–110.

[9] See Douglas Knight, *Pope and the Heroic Tradition* (New Haven, Yale University Press, 1951), pp. 34–39.

[10] For an account of how Dryden's satiric procedure draws upon "heroic" resources, see R. A. Brower, "An Allusion to Europe: Dryden and Tradition," *ELH,* XIX (1952), 38–48.

[11] I ignore the important "mock-epic" aspect of *The Rape of the Lock* both because it is so familiar and because I think a "pastoral" treatment gets closer to the heart of Pope's relation to his subject.

[12] William Empson, *Some Versions of Pastoral* (London, Chatto and Windus, 1935), pp. 11–12.

[13] For *The Rape of the Lock* as a comic treatment of serious sexual matters, see Cleanth Brooks, "The Case of Miss Arabella Fermor," in *The Well Wrought Urn* (London, D. Dobson, 1948), pp. 74–95.

[14] For the serious effect of the Homeric parody in Clarissa's speech, see Maynard Mack, "Wit and Poetry and Pope," in *Pope and His Contemporaries,* p. 37; and Brower, *Alexander Pope,* p. 161.

[15] Pope changed the original "Verses" to the more precise "Elegy" in the 1736 *Works.*

[16] For Ovidian elements in these poems, see Geoffrey Tillotson's introductions, *TE,* II, 275–291, 334–336; and Brower, *Alexander Pope,* pp. 63–84.

Chapter 2.

[1] For a strong refutation of "romantic" objections to didacticism per se, see Yvor Winters, *In Defense of Reason* (New York, Swallow Press and William Morrow, 1947), pp. 239–240.

[2] Reuben A. Brower, *Alexander Pope: The Poetry of Allusion* (Oxford, Clarendon Press, 1959), pp. 213–239, considers the *Essay on Man* as a version of the Horatian diatribe-epistle.

[3] Martin Price, *Swift's Rhetorical Art* (New Haven, Yale University Press, 1953), p. 65.

[4] For the "correspondences," see E. M. W. Tillyard, *The Elizabethan World Picture* (London, Chatto and Windus, 1943), pp. 77–93. Their breakdown in the eighteenth century is discussed by Earl R. Wasserman, "Nature Moralized: The Divine Analogy in the Eighteenth Century," *ELH,* XX (1953), 39–76.

[5] Alfred North Whitehead, *Science and the Modern World* (New York, Macmillan, 1925), p. 118.

[6] A. O. Lovejoy, "'Pride' in Eighteenth-Century Thought," in *Essays in the History of Ideas* (Baltimore, Johns Hopkins Press, 1948), p. 68.

[7] See A. O. Lovejoy, *The Great Chain of Being* (Cambridge, Mass., Harvard University Press, 1936), p. 202. My argument in this chapter owes much to this great work.

[8] For the difference between arguing from analogy and genuine analogical thinking, see S. L. Bethell, *The Cultural Revolution of the Seventeenth Century* (London, D. Dobson, 1951), chap. iii.

[9] *TE,* III (i), xxxiv–xxxv.

[10] Lovejoy, *The Great Chain of Being,* pp. 229–230.

[11] I adopt "externalistic pathos" from *ibid.,* pp. 11–12.

[12] Nov. 24, 1737; George Sherburn, *The Correspondence of Alexander Pope* (Oxford, Clarendon Press, 1956), IV, 89.

[13] "Argument of the Fourth Epistle," *TE,* III (i), 127.

[14] Joseph Addison, *The Spectator,* No. 62 (Friday, May 11, 1711).

[15] Whitehead, *Science and the Modern World,* p. 11.

[16] *TE,* III (i), lxxii.

CHAPTER 3.

[1] R. A. Brower, *The Fields of Light* (New York, Oxford University Press, 1951), p. 147, describes the clash between "the accent of Roman cultivation" and "backstairs vulgarity" in the *Epistle to Burlington.*

[2] Rebecca Price Parkin, *The Poetic Workmanship of Alexander Pope* (Minneapolis, University of Minnesota Press, 1955), pp. 223–230, discusses Pope's condemnation of "solipsism."

[3] *TE,* III (ii), 21n.

[4] Line numbers for the *Epistle to Bathurst* follow F. W. Bateson's welcome rearrangement of Warburton's "deathbed" text, in *TE,* III (ii).

[5] R. H. Tawney, *Religion and the Rise of Capitalism* (New York, Harcourt, Brace, 1926), p. 248.

[6] For the difference of view between Pope and Bathurst, and an elaborate reading of the poem in the light of Christian moral tradition, see Earl R. Wasserman (ed.), *Pope's Epistle to Bathurst* (Baltimore, Johns Hopkins Press, 1960), pp. 11–55.

[7] L. C. Knights, *Drama and Society in the Age of Jonson* (London, Chatto and Windus, 1937).

[8] To appreciate how remarkably Pope anticipates the social agonies of the next century, see Raymond Williams' brilliant *Culture and Society 1780–1950* (London, Chatto and Windus, 1958), especially some of the commentary on Ruskin, pp. 138–146.

[9] Here I am in disagreement with Mr. Brower (*Alexander Pope,* pp. 251, 258–260) and with Paul J. Alpers, "Pope's *To Bathurst* and the Mandevillian State," *ELH,* XXV (1958), 23–42, though my discussion of the point may suggest that our differences are more terminological than substantial.

[10] Max Weber, *The Protestant Ethic and the Spirit of Capitalism,* tr. Talcott Parsons (New York, Scribner's, 1930), p. 71.

[11] Kenneth Burke, *Permanence and Change,* (2d. ed.; Los Altos, Calif., Hermes Publications, 1954), p. 42.

[12] *Summa Theologica,* 2^a 2^{ae}, Q. lxxxiii, art. vi., quoted by Tawney, *Religion and the Rise of Capitalism,* p. 32.

[13] William Empson, *Seven Types of Ambiguity* (2d. ed.; London, Chatto and Windus, 1947), pp. 150–151.

CHAPTER 4.

[1] Quoted by Ian Jack, *Augustan Satire* (Oxford, Clarendon Press, 1952), p. 103.

[2] Reuben A. Brower, *Alexander Pope: The Poetry of Allusion* (Oxford, Clarendon Press, 1959), pp. 287–288, suggests that Horace himself was on occasion "un-Horatian" in a Juvenalian way.

[3] *The Works of Alexander Pope,* ed. Whitwell Elwin and W. J. Courthope (London, J. Murray, 1871–1889), X, 551.

[4] William Empson, *Some Versions of Pastoral* (London, Chatto and Windus, 1935), pp. 11–12.

[5] I adopt the useful term *adversarius* from Mary Claire Randolph, "The Structural Design of the Formal Verse Satire," *Philological Quarterly,* XXI (1942), 372.

[6] *TE,* IV, 327n.

[7] Henry James, Preface to *The Lesson of the Master,* in *The Art of the Novel,* ed. R. P. Blackmur (New York, Scribner's, 1934), p. 222.

[8] Kenneth Burke, *Attitudes Toward History* (2d. ed.; Los Altos, Calif., Hermes Publications, 1959), pp. 59–60.

[9] For a perceptive view of the poem's organization, see D. J. Greene, " 'Logical Structure' in Eighteenth-Century Poetry," *Philological Quarterly,* XXI (1952), 330–331.

[10] Gilbert Wakefield, *Observations on Pope* (London, 1796), p. 233.

[11] Maynard Mack (ed.), *The Augustans* (New York, Prentice-Hall, 1950), p. 30.

[12] Mack, "Wit and Poetry and Pope," in *Pope and His Contemporaries: Essays Presented to George Sherburn,* ed. J. L. Clifford and L. A. Landa (Oxford, Clarendon Press, 1949), p. 36.

[13] For representative views of the persona, see Elder Olson, "Rhetoric and the Appreciation of Pope," *Modern Philology,* XXXVII (1939), 13–35; and Maynard Mack, "The Muse of Satire," *Yale Review,* XLI (1951), 83.

[14] F. R. Leavis, *The Common Pursuit* (London, Chatto and Windus, 1952), p. 86.

CHAPTER 5.

[1] Aubrey L. Williams, *Pope's Dunciad: A Study of Its Meaning* (Baton Rouge, Louisiana State University Press, 1955).

[2] For this parody, see Geoffrey Tillotson, *On the Poetry of Pope* (2d. ed.; Oxford, Clarendon Press, 1950), p. 155.

[3] F. R. Leavis, *The Common Pursuit* (London, Chatto and Windus, 1952), p. 90.

[4] Although my treatment of light and darkness in the *Dunciad* is not indebted to them, I should mention the interesting comments on the subject by G. Wilson Knight in *Laureate of Peace* (London, Routledge and Kegan Paul, 1954), pp. 57–58, and Rebecca Price Parkin in *The Poetic Workmanship of Alexander Pope* (Minneapolis, University of Minnesota Press, 1955), pp. 116–123. For complaints that the poem lacks unity, see Tillotson, *On the Poetry of Pope,* p. 58, and Ian Jack, *Augustan Satire* (Oxford, Clarendon Press, 1952), pp. 125–126.

[5] There is a cluster of images here that Pope was remarkably fond of; for a discussion, see T. R. Edwards, Jr., "The Colors of Fancy: An Image Cluster in Pope," *Modern Language Notes,* LXXIII (1958), 485–489.

[6] When the poem was exclusively about bad writers, it was "wit" that finally was engulfed in darkness: "*Let there be darkness!* (the dread pow'r shall say) / All shall be darkness, as it ne'er were Day; / To their first Chaos Wit's vain works shall fall, / And universal Dulness cover all!" All the 1728 editions have this reading; although Pope made the major revisions for the first Variorum edition (1729), their full import becomes clear only in the context of the 1743 version.

[7] Though it is possible to take lines 651–652 as parallel, "public" going with "human" and "private" with "divine," I read "human Spark" as including both the kinds of "flame" mentioned in 651, so that "Glimpse divine" adds a new term.

[8] Compare "As things seem large which we thro' Mists descry, / *Dulness* is ever apt to Magnify" (*Essay on Criticism,* 392–393). The *Dunciad* shows Pope reconsidering the confident association of light and nature made in the *Essay.*

[9] Marjorie Nicolson, *Newton Demands the Muse* (Princeton, Princeton University Press, 1946), p. 52, quotes Locke, Berkeley, and Addison on sight as the most important sense.

[10] Thomas De Quincey, "Pope," in *Works* (Edinburgh, 1863), XV, 134.

[11] For the story, and Aubrey's efforts to refute it, see D. G. James, *The Life of Reason* (London, Longmans, Green, 1949), p. 7.

[12] Joseph Spence, *Observations, Anecdotes, and Characters of Books and Men* (London, 1858), pp. 150, 158.

[13] William Empson, *The Structure of Complex Words* (London, Chatto and Windus, 1951), p. 92.

[14] A. O. Lovejoy, *Essays in the History of Ideas* (Baltimore, Johns Hopkins Press, 1948), p. 80.

[15] Leavis, *The Common Pursuit,* p. 91.

[16] See Williams, *Pope's Dunciad,* p. 139, for *Paradise Lost* II, 980–986 as a key to Pope's emphasis on original darkness. (All italics in this paragraph are mine.)

CONCLUSION

[1] See Basil Willey, *The Eighteenth Century Background* (London, Chatto and Windus, 1940), pp. 1–2.

[2] Louis I. Bredvold, "The Gloom of the Tory Satirists," in *Pope and His Contemporaries,* pp. 1–19, points out that darkness of mood characterized the writings of Pope's whole literary circle, and ascribes the fact to politically motivated distaste for "the declining moral tone of England under Walpole." Just as I dissent from Mr. Bredvold's belief that "even the darkest page of Swift leaves us with [a] feeling of soundness at the core," so I must say that Pope's "satiric" gloom and disgust seem to me too powerfully stated to be merely political protest.

[3] Invaluable material for a revised view of eighteenth-century literature is contained in Ernest Tuveson's *The Imagination as a Means of Grace* (Berkeley and Los Angeles, University of California Press, 1960), though I should insist that Pope comes perilously close to the "breakdown of the sense of value in the cosmos, and of confidence in the dignity of man" which Mr. Tuveson (p. 67) says did not occur until the next century.

[4] See, for example, Mark Schorer, *William Blake* (New York, Henry Holt, 1946), pp. 31–33, 38–39; and Northrop Frye, *Fearful Symmetry* (Princeton, Princeton University Press, 1947), pp. 161–168. In fairness, it should be noted that Mr. Frye explains that his summary of Blake's view of the Augustans is in some ways "caricature."

[5] D. G. James, *The Romantic Comedy* (London, Oxford University Press, 1948), pp. 1–63.

[6] Austin Warren, *Rage for Order* (Chicago, University of Chicago Press, 1948), p. 50.

[7] W. B. Yeats, "The Circus Animals' Desertion," *The Collected Poems of W. B. Yeats* (New York, Macmillan, 1956), p. 336.